How to AVOID a Drunk Driving CONVICTION

Judge X

Loompanics Unlimited
Port Townsend, Washington

NOTICE TO READERS:

We have made every effort to provide you with the best information available at the time of writing. However, drunk driving laws are constantly being analyzed and changed, and the laws are enforced differently in each jurisdiction. We encourage you to check with the proper authorities in your area to determine the current status of these laws.

This book is sold for information purposes only. If you want legal advice, please consult an attorney. Neither the author nor the publisher will be held accountable for the use or misuse of the information contained in this book.

Published by:
Loompanics Unlimited
P.O. Box 1197
Port Townsend, WA 98368

Cover photo: © David R. Frazier/West Stock

ISBN 1-55950-093-X
Library of Congress Catalog Card Number 92-75832

Loompanics Unlimited is a division of Loompanics Enterprises, Inc.

Contents

GENDER DISCLAIMER

The world of drunk drivers is populated mostly by men. Male drivers, cops, lawyers and judges dominate the system with occasional female interlopers slipping into each category. That is why, throughout this book, I mostly refer to people as he and him, and their possessions as his. Not only does it make for an easier read, but it generally speaks the truth. In the world of drunk drivers, men are much more often the culpricks... and no, I am not a dyke.

Coulda been the whiskey
Mighta been the gin
Coulda been the three or four six-packs,
I don't know
But look at the mess I'm in.
> *Wasn't it a Party*
> **The Irish Rovers**

"I had to drive home, your honor, I was too drunk to walk."
> — **A Drunk Driver's Defense**

"Even a goddamn werewolf is entitled to legal representation."
> — **Doctor Gonzo**
> The Samoan Lawyer
> *Fear and Loathing in Las Vegas*
> Hunter S. Thompson

INTRODUCTION

Now comes Miller time.

The boss has been a tyrant all day, but in two minutes, you'll be out of here. The gang has already gone out to the roadhouse. A couple beers on the way home is just the right idea.

You drink light beer, three of them, lower in calories and alcoholic content than regular beer. They hardly put a glow on your otherwise sober complexion.

Before you leave, the bartender refills the half-empty bowl of trail-mix munchies on the bar, and you grab another handful to compensate for the lunch you didn't eat.

It's 5:25 p.m., almost dark. You loosen your shirt and tie, gulp the last few ounces of beer, wave at the gang and head for the car, home and dinner. You're sober.

You're only a hundred yards down the highway when a police car suddenly appears behind you. The light goes on and you pull over. What the hell... ambushed? But it's O.K. You're sober.

The officer approaches and you wind down the window.

"Know ya got a flickerin' tail light there, fella? Let's see your driver's license and registration."

You fish your license out of a wallet full of credit cards, but where the hell is the registration? You fumble in the glove compartment, look above the visor, search the dashboard. No luck.

"Uh... musta... uh... guess... guess I left it at home," you mumble.

The cop nods and squints. Here it comes. "You been drinkin', fella?"

Damn. Can't lie, he saw you pull out of the roadhouse. The cop's a damn bounty hunter. You shrug.

"Step outta the car, fella. I'm gonna do a few tests."

You carefully step onto the road berm, avoiding the larger stones mixed in the gravel. The hassle is getting you angry. There is no reason for this. You're sober.

"Count to ten," he says.

You show him. You count to fourteen and he stops you. He places three coins on the ground in front of you, each coin spaced about eighteen inches apart.

"Pick 'em up," he says.

Hell, you can do this with one easy stretch. You bend and snatch the first coin, swing over and grab the second, then reach for the third but one coin falls out of your hand on the last snatch. You sigh, stretch further, reach for the two coins laying together. You make the pick-up, but your knee touches the ground and you have to push off with your free hand.

The cop nods as you hand him back the coins. He points toward the police car.

"Walk heel-to-toe past the patrol car and back."

"I oughta run," you think. "Show 'em some heels alright. What a bunch of B.S."

You walk in a hurry to the end of the police car, turn and walk back swinging your arms and breathing hard. You are really getting pissed.

"O.K., buddy. Lock your car, and we'll go to the station for a breath test. I think you had a little too much to drink; you flunked all three of my field tests."

You sit on a hard chair in the interview room, waiting for the breath machine to warm-up. You barely answered the interviewer's questions (Are you on any medication? When did you eat last?).

You are smoldering angry. It's almost 7:00 p.m. and your wife is gonna kill you. For Christ's sake, three light beers, you were sober!

The machine signals ready and the operator points to the newly attached plastic mouthpiece on the intake tube. (Blow hard? Blow easy? Screw it, just blow, you *know* you're sober.)

You blow into the machine, it beeps a couple times, you wait a minute, then blow again. The machine growls to itself for a moment, then spits out a card with your test scores: .09 on the first blow, .08 on the second.

Did you pass?

Well... In many jurisdictions, you would have, but not yours. Your State Legislature recently enacted the two-beer standard for drunk driving, lowering the blood alcohol content required for conviction from .10 to .08.

You are no longer sober. Welcome to the ranks of the most popular criminals in America: Drunk Drivers.

You have the right to remain silent. Call your wife. Have her bring three hundred dollars bail to the station, and she can take you home.

You have the right to a lawyer. The hearing is at 10:00 a.m. next Tuesday at the magistrate's office. You'd better get that lawyer, fella. You could go to jail for this.

According to standard police testimony, the prototype drunk driver has "a strong odor of alcoholic beverage on his breath, disheveled clothing, a flushed face, glassy eyes, slurred or confused speech and is uncoordinated and unable to follow directions." With this information in mind, let's do a quick study on why the driver in the opening scenario got arrested.

Odor. The driver lowered his window only when the officer approached his vehicle. The concentration of alcoholic odor was intensified in the enclosed vehicle and exploded on the officer when the window was lowered. Even had the driver *not* been drinking, the tell-tale stink of stale barroom smoke and beer on his clothing would have signaled the officer a warning. A driver's odor is the first sign that cops search for and recognize at any traffic stop or accident. There are secrets to neutralizing odor at a traffic stop. They work for off-duty cops. They can work for you as well.

Disheveled Clothing. All cops testify to disheveled clothing, but few know what it is. Here, the driver had loosened his shirt and tie. That counts toward disheveled clothing testimony at trial. Remember, the cop's testimony is looked at by most judges in a light most favorable to the prosecution. That's why, within reason, cops can lie their asses off and get away with it. A driver doesn't have to puke on himself to have disheveled clothing. A loose tie or a shirttail hanging out comes into evidence as a mark against you. Neatness counts, but I honest to God don't know why. From what I see *inside* the barrooms, slobs with earrings get the prettiest girls.

Flushed face, glassy eyes. The driver here fell into a classic cop trap. When ambushed for no apparent reason, he got cocky and angry. His emotions gave him the appearance of a drunk. Dumb. Even though cops can always find a reason to stop you, this was a non-custodial stop and the driver was not under arrest. His anger and attitude got him into court. Worse, at the time of his traffic stop, he really *wasn't* legally drunk *yet.*

Slurred, confused speech. A driver doesn't need to speak like a deaf-mute to fail this test. Delayed answers, shrugs, a pause and an "Ahh"..., these observations by the cop argue for closer inspection and further testing. Here, our driver was flustered when he couldn't find or remember where his registration card was located. Because he wasn't prepared for the officer's routine questions and paper requests, the bombshell question that followed (You been drinkin' fella?) left him speechless. His answer was a shrug and one thing you cannot do *ever* is shrug off a traffic cop.

Uncoordinated, unable to follow directions. These observations usually flow from the field sobriety test after the driver is *asked* out of his vehicle. The cop always wins a field sobriety test because he assesses the grade. Our angry, cocky, *sober* driver in this instance actually flunked all three field tests simply by not following directions. Cops are sort of a half-assed military mob, so when a cop gives a field test order, he wants *precise* compliance. I am bewildered and amazed when a wise guy shows off for the cop and then gets arrested only because he didn't follow directions. Our man in this instance was *asked* to count to ten, not fourteen; he was *asked* to pick up three coins *in any manner* he chose (he chose poorly); and he was *asked* to walk past the police car and back, not just to the rear fender and return. Even sober, he still failed the field sobriety test that he was *asked* to perform. There are two quick notes here. First, when a cop *asks* you to perform a field sobriety test, he's probably already decided that there is sufficient cause to take you in for a chemical test to determine your blood alcohol content. He's now looking for that last nail to seal your coffin.

Second, I italicize *ask* because a cop cannot compel you to take a field test and cannot punish you for a refusal. But! Don't confuse this with refusal to take a chemical test: blood, breath or urine. You *will* be penalized for a chemical test refusal under the implied consent statutes.

By now you should begin to see that drunk driving takes a little prior planning. First, have your seat belt buckled. It shows the cop that you were at least *thinking* safety. Now, when the cop approaches, your hands should be high on the wheel, your window should already be down, your driver's license and owner's cards ready and a little smile on your face: "Hi officer." You have now relaxed the cop, assured him of his safety and impressed him with your preparedness. If this is a routine traffic stop, the cop is not now thinking "Drunk Driver." You're halfway home.

In the following format of questions and answers, I will give you information, legal and otherwise, that will aid you in avoiding a drunk driving conviction. (Never mind the funny numbers after the court cases I have cited; that's for your lawyer. All you need to know is the substance of the law and that is what I have provided.) But, keep in mind that this information is not absolute. Laws change (especially with the pro-police Supreme Court in power now), and some people just can't be taught. No advice can help the maniac who drinks grain alcohol and kool-aid all day then blasts off for the night life, northbound on the southbound expressway.

But there is such a thing as a reasonably prudent drunk driver, and he or she is the focus of this book. I know the Mothers Against Drunk Drivers, a hundred million dollars strong, will be screaming for my anonymous head, but the statistics bear me out. Ten years ago, the predominant blood alcohol standard nationwide for presumptive drunk driving was .15 percent. Today, the standard has been generally lowered to .10 and is a lock to soon hit .08 (the two beer standard) in many states. So what was just drunk driving ten years ago is often double drunk driving today. The measuring stick has gotten a lot shorter.

Still, booze sells like crazy. The United States' average consumption per capita of beer alone in 1990 was about 25 gallons.

Did you ever wonder how Norm Peterson gets home from *Cheers?* If he drove, even once, he's a real criminal under the new standards. All across America, there are taverns along the roads and highways. Convenience stores at the Interstate exits sell beer and wine, packaged to go. Even in the heart of Baptist abstinence, Corbin, Kentucky, where it's a sixty mile hike in any direction for a legal drink, there are nine alcohol recovery centers in town. And here's a chilling thought for you. On any given Saturday night in America, there are over a million drunk drivers on the highways.

But the people who make the laws realize that every driver who exceeds the blood alcohol standard is not an automatic menace. That's why many states' drunk driving codes require the police officer to testify, *in addition* to the driver's blood alcohol level, that from the officer's trained observations, he has formed the opinion that the driver was incapable of safe driving and created a hazard to himself and others. Even in a per se jurisdiction, (every state except Kentucky, Maryland, Massachusetts, Tennessee, South Carolina and Puerto Rico), where a blood alcohol reading in excess of the legal limit may stand alone and convict a driver without the officer's testimony, often that is the law but not the practice. Similar to the prosecution of the 55 mph speeding law, cops, judges and prosecutors sometimes recognize a tolerable blood alcohol level above the statutory limit. I know many police officers and municipal court judges who, unless there was an accident, either won't file or will summarily dismiss any drunk driving charge under .15. So what many people who work in the system are saying is: "There is such a thing as a reasonably prudent drunk driver."

Q & A With Judge X

Now, let's get on with learning everything you always wanted to know about avoiding a drunk driving conviction, but were afraid to ask your lawyer. First question.

What's the big deal about a drunk driving conviction? I pay a fine, right?

For a first offense, fines and costs (not including attorney's fees) are in the range of $1,000; in some states you could do a little jail time. But let's dig a little deeper. As another part of the sentence, there is usually a probation period of a year or so, a driver's license suspension up to a year, mandatory driving school classes and an order to do community service. Judges feel it is appropriate that criminal defendants recognize their misdeeds and visibly atone for them. Forty hours of cleaning toilets at the YMCA fits the bill nicely.

Sometimes you can plead through a drunk driving charge without a lawyer. When you can't, figure $1,500 — $5,000 in legal fees.

There are other considerations. Soon after your state's traffic bureau records a drunk driving conviction against you, the traffic bureau's computer talks to your insurance company's computer, giving notice of the bust. (Remember when you gave your date of birth, social security and driver's license number to your insurance agent? He wasn't asking because he wanted to send you a birthday card. *His* bosses wanted the information to index into the state's computer for a profitable occasion such as this.) You are now recorded as an alcohol related offender, a very dangerous risk for your insurance company. Your coverage will now either be canceled, placed in an assigned risk pool or recomputed to compensate for the risk. A good guess is that your insurance premium will double, *if* they keep you. But wait! Like a ginzu knife commercial, there's more!

Now the media bastards get to criminalize your name in print and on the air. It's not bad enough that the National Criminal Information Center (N.C.I.C.) has imaged your record forever (the F.B.I. packrats never expunge anything), now the newspaper will inform your friends, family, neighbors, enemies and employers that you are a criminal drunk. People have been fired for less, or at least sent to a rehabilitation center to clean-up for a month. Take my word for it, rehab is not a resort.

At the Betty Ford Alcoholic Recovery and Treatment Center, rehabilitation begins with toilet training... learning to clean them. You want on-the-job punishment?

Consider the National Football League's policy for *first-time* football player drunk drivers: A fine by the league president and a four-game suspension. This is in addition to what the courts do and probably much worse.

Athlete's salaries being what they are, a four-game suspension can amount to a couple hundred thousand dollar fine. Now there's a penalty to gladden some MADD hearts.

Now, saving the absolute worst for last, what if your drunk driving conviction arose from a fatal accident? Vehicular homicide almost always carries a mandatory term of years in prison. I peg the average at a minimum three years, no cut, hard time. It's a world of numbers; and operator license numbers and prisoner I.D. numbers are sometimes interchangeable.

Why are the drunk driving laws so tough? I mean, booze is everywhere.

The Federal Government, through pressure tactics, has coaxed the states to toughen their drunk driving laws over the past few years. Don't ask why, try Bud Dry, then chalk it up to another example of your tax dollars at work.

It looks like the Feds are moving toward a national driver's license, preempting the states and standardizing all traffic laws state-to-state. They have already started the process for commercial drivers. The idea behind a federally-monitored system is to close the loopholes in the differing reciprocal agreements between states. (Here's a little secret even though outside of our drunk driving subject.) Other states usually don't reciprocate points to your home state, because of the potential legal and administrative headaches involved. If you are a New York driver caught in Virginia for speeding, New York will suspend your license *only* for non-payment of the Virginia fine. Once the fine is paid, the substance of the violation is ignored. Many states, for the same administrative reasons, won't reciprocate probationary sentences for drunk driving. You can serve a silent probation in absentia and the conviction won't follow you home unless you were fingerprinted and your state accesses the National Computer on a later arrest.

If a conviction does follow you across state lines, you can probably have it upset by going to court in your home state and challenging the out-of-state conviction. The other state then must send a registrar from their motor vehicle department to certify your conviction and testify about the differences between the two state's point systems and motor vehicle codes. It becomes one big jerk-off and that is why states don't chase drivers for anything but money.

Here's a neat trick I learned from a cop who was denied professional courtesy and ticketed for speeding by another cop out-of-state. When the first summons for non-payment of fine and costs was delivered by certified mail from the out-of-state driver's license bureau, my friend marked the front of the envelope "deceased" and returned it to the mailman. A clerk back in the bureau promptly marked the ticket as uncollectible and no further action was taken.

You can see how a centralized system will put everyone under one big eye and close out most administrative opportunities for avoiding prosecution. In the example above, your home state's computer will just snitch on you to the Big Boss Computer. This would be particularly damaging to repeat drunk drivers. It's possible now to have several prior convictions out-of-state yet be recorded in a new state as a first-time offender. Under a national system, all prior convictions would be automatically available to cops and courts without request.

If I have a couple beers on the way home from work, does that really make me a drunk driver?

Drunk driving is generally described as operating or being in physical control of a vehicle on a public trafficway *while under the influence of alcohol to a degree which renders the driver incapable of safe driving.* Note that under this definition *all* instances of driving under the influence do not constitute drunk driving. Even in those per se jurisdictions where any driving while above the state's blood alcohol standard is enough by itself to convict, an alcohol reading below the standard does not then constitute drunk driving.

If you have three or four beers (figure 12 oz. bottles) on the way home, you have to consider a few circumstances before forming your own opinion of whether you are legally drunk.

First, did you eat lunch? Food slows down the absorption rate of alcohol into the blood stream, through the liver and particularly through the stomach wall. You can get drunk on a few drinks quickly if you haven't eaten. When you're hauled in for a chemical test, this is one of the first questions the interviewer will ask: When and what did you last eat? Here the interviewer means a regular meal, not the beef jerky, two blind robins and bag of beer nuts you gobbled while drinking.

Years ago I received some good advice from an old Mustache Pete at an Italian wedding who watched me gyrate through a series of purple heaves from too much Dago Red: "Hey, iffa you gonna drink, you's gotta eat."

Next consider *what* you have been drinking. Light beer packs less wallop than high-test, especially imports. I submit with some assurance that four bottles of Beck's Dark consumed on an empty stomach is going to put you in harm's way. Dorothy Parker was correct when she said, "Liquor does it quicker." Hair spray can inebriate in two or three whiffs. Chug mouthwash (26.9%) and you don't need whiskey, but your breath will smell fresh. The "experts" have figured that a regular 12 oz. beer packs the same alcoholic wallop as a 4 oz. glass of wine or a 1½ oz. shot of whiskey. Considering most factors, on a .10 standard, a 160 pound person should be legally drunk after drinking five drinks within an hour. The general advisory is, if you must drink and drive, limit your drinks to one per hour. Check out the chart shown in Figure 1, but know that it is based on an "average" computed from several other "averages" based on a single, controlled experiment sixty years ago (with men only) involving only one kind of drinking scenario (empty stomach absorption). Naturally, it has become the law for presumptive intoxication levels in almost every state.

Now let's break the "drunk driver" definition down a little further. If you leave the bar, get in your vehicle, start it, then get woozy and lay down for a few minutes, you are probably subject to arrest for drunk driving without even driving! The tavern's parking lot is open to the public and is therefore considered a trafficway. Since you let the engine run, you are in actual physical control of the vehicle. Parked, sleeping drivers

Drinks	APPROXIMATE BLOOD ALCOHOL PERCENTAGE Body Weight in Pounds							
	100	120	140	160	180	200	220	240
1	.038	.031	.027	.023	.021	.019	.017	.016
2	.075	.063	.054	.047	.042	.038	.034	.031
3	.113	.094	.080	.070	.063	.056	.051	.047
4	.150	.125	.107	.094	.083	.075	.068	.063
5	.188	.156	.134	.117	.104	.094	.085	.078
6	.225	.188	.161	.141	.125	.113	.102	.094
7	.263	.219	.188	.164	.146	.131	.119	.109
8	.300	.250	.214	.188	.167	.150	.136	.125
9	.338	.281	.241	.211	.188	.169	.153	.141
10	.375	.313	.268	.234	.208	.188	.170	.156

Figure 1

are routinely convicted of drunk driving if the key is in the ignition without the engine running, even if parked off the road. If you "feel" drunk, then, by all means, get the hell off the road. I mean *all the way off the road* where you are not a hazard, even to other drunk drivers who can find and bang into you almost anywhere. Next, park and lock your vehicle from the inside, kill the engine, *pull the keys and hide them,* then climb in the back seat and sleep it off. Never say "never," but under any laws I know about, you have now secured yourself against a drunk driving arrest.

***What do I do if I've been drinking and a cop stops me?
Blast off, right?***

It's a very unwise decision to elude the police officer once
you have been signaled to pull over. You risk *real* jail time by
blasting off. And car chases promote violence. A wild ride about
town that results in a traffic fatality will certainly meet the legal
standard of gross negligence needed to convict an otherwise
just drunk driver of vehicular homicide. You are talking
penitentiary time on this one. Further, a fleeing driver risks getting a "bristol stomp" when finally apprehended. Cops who
chase fleeing drivers feel they have a special right to use
"necessary force to effect the arrest" once the driver is pulled
from the car. Somebody is going to get the shit kicked out of
them.

In my twenty-odd years as a judge, I have seen hundreds of
bloodied men and women hauled into night court, shackled,
ahead of smirking cops who only mutter "Resisted," when
questioned about the bloodshed. I can't remember a car chase
defendant who ever came before me unmarked. A fleeing driver
is always construed as resisting arrest. If you are going to run,
run for your life. The life you save may be your own. But don't
blame me when the cops blow your shit away. You asked for it.

Really. If an officer signals you, don't panic. Let him know
immediately by waving your hand (use *all* of your fingers) that
you have seen him and intend to comply. This assures him that
you are not a criminal type and he is reasonably safe at this
traffic stop. You must act sober. Remember, all the best actors
aren't in Hollywood. Be decent, the cop may not *yet* suspect you
of drunk driving. Perhaps your car really does have a flickering
taillight.

Now pull off the road *slowly* at the first *safe* place where you
and the cop are not both in jeopardy of the next approaching
drunk driver. *And get your window down.* Remember, out goes

the bad air, in comes the good air and the sooner, the better. Also, a quick spray from a can of air freshener is not illegal, even if it's a little much to ask. Always have your cards close and ready so that the cop can't testify later that you were "fumbling and uncoordinated." Finally, get your hands up on the wheel where the cop can see them as he approaches. Remember, the cop is not first thinking "drunk driver," he's thinking "gun"! Now, relax and shut up. The cop *must* have a legal reason for stopping you and he will tell you about it. This is called probable cause and even the present Supreme Court hasn't changed the law as it applies to traffic stops. Here is your proof: "A motorist surrenders neither his reasonable expectations of privacy nor the protections of the Fourth Amendment (right to be free from unreasonable search and seizure) when he steps into his automobile." *Delaware v. Prouse,* 440 U.S. 648 (1979). Note that this applies to a traffic stop, not a drunk driving checkpoint which I will cover later.

At this point, the law is still on your side. A cop has a right, for safety and investigative reasons, to order you out of the car, but you are not yet under arrest and your only other obligation is to show the cop your driver's license and vehicle-related cards. The cop needs *individualized suspicion* to get the arrest treadmill working. It is important now that you smell good. Cops who drink and drive use Hall's Mentholyptus. Not only is it an excellent breath masking agent, it can, in some circumstances, screw up the breathalyzer readings on older equipment, causing too wide a variance in the test results so that the results may be unreliable as evidence. Further, the medicinal odor makes you believable when you avoid the cop's questions by pointing to your throat and faking laryngitis.

If the traffic stop is routine and the cop isn't faking probable cause, agree with whatever he says. Nod. Don't argue with him! It is truly amazing that people will engage in loud and violent argument with someone who is wearing a gun. If the cop suspects you of drinking, he will either accuse you immediately or look for evidence in your car (open bottles, beer cans, coolers) while he questions you and smells you up. While it is *not* against the law to drink and drive since all drinking does not constitute drunkenness, it is generally against the law to drink *while* driving... and it is probable cause by itself to make a traffic stop. If you drink *while* driving, stop reading my advice, put your hands over your head and give yourself up. No matter what I tell you, sooner or later you are going to be arrested.

But... if you insist, you must hide the booze before the cop gets to you, and this isn't all that easy. Cops have all kinds of crazy lights, and they are watching your every move. Keep a bag, box or *closed* container near you and quickly place your drink inside, then close or cover it so the cop can't see inside the bag or box. Don't spill it, the police dog has a good nose. Even on an investigative stop, the cop can only make a search of your vehicle of articles *in plain view*. Do not hide the booze on your person. The cop is permitted to frisk you for a weapon. Any booze or dope he finds on you goes along with the territory. You're busted.

It's a favorite cop trick to ask your permission to do a vehicle search. Don't consent, ever. You have a privacy right, so protect it, even if you have nothing to hide.

Otherwise, if you have passed the cop's odor test and your driving wasn't altogether maniacal, you are probably soon going to be back on the highway. Even alcoholic odor by itself is not sufficient probable cause to request a field sobriety test since the odor of alcohol on your breath has nothing to do with your ability to safely drive a vehicle. The cop has to accumulate all the circumstances which make him believe that you are an unsafe driver, then he goes for proof that you are drunk by way of field sobriety tests and a chemical test of your blood. His best circumstance is usually the actual reason for which he stopped you... your driving sucks. Remember! You have no obligation to take a field sobriety test or a preliminary breath test, and you cannot be punished for a refusal.

What do I tell the cop if he asks if I've been drinking?

Lawyers used to advise their clients to tell the truth, then lie: "Yes, officer, I've been drinking. I had two beers." But a driver's admissions, even from a general, non-custodial, on the scene interview, may be used against him. If you tell the cop that you were drinking, you will almost certainly get a chemical test. If you lie, he has to form an independent opinion from all the other circumstances. This is important, particularly at a drunk driving roadblock, where everyone stopped is asked if they have been drinking. There is no individualized suspicion.

Remember that the Fifth Amendment guarantees you the right to remain silent. You don't have to tell the cop anything. But if push comes to shove, you have one clear option. Ask if you are under arrest. If the cop says "No," you are free to leave without answering the question. If he has arrested you already, the arrest is so premature that his case against you is probably in jeopardy... *AND*... if you are now under arrest, the cop has to read you your Miranda rights which explicitly give you the right to remain silent. So, from a legal standpoint, when asked if you have been drinking, is your best answer "No"? Well, it would probably be the answer I'd give, although I've never been arrested, and I drink and drive three times a week. But there is a real danger here. If you lie and the chemical test proves you were drinking, your lie will come into evidence as a fatal blow to your credibility. You will be destroyed at trial. Isn't it interesting how our legal system makes you just want to tell the truth, no matter how much it hurts?

Here is a standard prosecutor's checklist of factors indicative of intoxication that a police officer will be questioned about in court.

- Odor of alcohol

- Bloodshot or watery eyes

- Defective balance (staggering, stumbling, swaying)

- Disarranged or soiled clothing

- Flushed or pale face

- Slurred, mumbled, confused or incoherent speech

- Lack of dexterity

- Impaired memory, awareness or orientation

- Impaired judgment

- Insensibility to pain

- Unusual attitude — cocky, sleepy, combative, indifferent, angry, hilarious

- Unusual acts — vomiting, belching, hiccuping, taking a dump in pants

Figure 2

What if the cop didn't read me my rights, do I win?

In *Berkemer v. McCarty*, 468 U.S., 104 S. Ct. 1136, 82 L.Ed. 2d 317 (1984), the United States Supreme Court ruled that a roadside questioning of a motorist detained at a routine traffic stop does not constitute custodial interrogation and therefore does not require the reading of Miranda rights. Your Miranda rights include the right to remain silent, the right to have a lawyer and the right not to give certain evidence against yourself. The Supreme Court has side-stepped this by recognizing that custody can begin *after* all the physical evidence has been collected. You don't have the right to call your lawyer until after you have taken a chemical test. You *always* have the right to remain silent but the cops don't have to tell you until they arrest you and they don't have to arrest you until after the blood alcohol test has been taken. If the cop does read you your rights prior to the blood alcohol test, you now have the right to call your lawyer and get advice whether you should take the test. Further, the cop now has to tell you that the Miranda warnings he just gave you have no bearing on your right to refuse a blood alcohol test. He must tell you that your test refusal stands alone and Miranda, for alcohol test purposes only, cannot be used as an excuse not to take the test. It is imperative you know *when* and *if* you are arrested, so ask. A final note on rights: Even though you may not be arrested until the very end of the process, you can still be held by the police for chemical testing. You agreed to this by "implied consent" when you applied for your driver's license. The court reasoned that a driver's license is a privilege, not a right, so you either consent to an alcohol test or lose the privilege of driving.

Say what? I never agreed to nothin'. What the hell is implied consent?

In a maneuver around your right not to give evidence against yourself, the states have individually adopted some form of an implied consent statute where you trade off this right as a pre-condition to the issuance of a driver's license. The police then have the right to ask you, upon probable cause, to perform a chemical test by giving a blood, breath or urine sample. You *still* have a corresponding right to refuse the request, *BUT...* you will be punished under the statute for refusing. Most sanctions for refusal are administrative, which means that the state will yank your driver's license, usually for a year, upon a refusal. But several states have criminalized the process, making it a misdemeanor if you refuse a blood, breath or urine test. Additionally, many states permit the officer to double-charge for the offense of drunk driving plus the refusal, whether administrative or criminal. If the cop charges you with drunk driving after a refusal, his case is more difficult to prove because he has to show drunk driving from the surrounding circumstances (your refusal, your odor and appearance, the nature of the stop and his general observations). Still, he's got nothing to lose by charging you with D.U.I. on top of a refusal because he's already got one win. He's taken your driver's license. And cops are awfully trigger-happy when it comes to reaching a conclusion that you refused. As well, courts have shown little sympathy for the refusing motorist. Repeated requests to call a lawyer before taking a chemical test have been ruled a refusal. Failure to supply enough breath for the test and refusal to sign hospital consent forms have also been upheld as refusals. Anything substantially less than an unqualified, unequivocal assent to take a chemical test constitutes a refusal.

But there are a few rules of the road to guide you. Generally, if a cop asks you to take a chemical test, you should take it, especially if this is your first offense. There are alternative sentencing programs for first offenders which are not as punitive as the penalty for a refusal. We'll talk about that later.

For repeat offenders, a refusal is probably a good idea because your license is already damaged and in jeopardy and the subsequent grading of a new offense may put you into a felony drunk driving category. If you are looking at real jail time, there is no sense in helping the cop make his case. In states that have criminalized refusal, you don't really have an option, since you are going to get routed to criminal court either way.

If you drink and drive, you should know your state's law. Call Triple A, a defense lawyer, the police station (no kidding), the local court or your state's traffic safety bureau and ask what the penalties are for a refusal. Are they criminal or administrative? How long is a license suspended under the implied consent statute? It's better to know before you go. Why learn bad news from the cop? In the back of this book, you will find an appendix that gives you the state-to-state blood-alcohol levels required for conviction and other related drunk driving information. It's a start.

Finally, we turn from bad news to tragic. If you are involved in an accident, whether it is your fault or another's, and there is *any* possibility that someone is going to die, do not, under any circumstances that you control, do not, do not, do not take a chemical test. We are talking about *years* of your life in jail here on a conviction for Homicide by Vehicle. An underlying conviction for drunk driv-ing goes a long way toward establishing the gross negligence issue needed to convict you on the homicide charge. It doesn't matter that you didn't *want* to kill anybody. Your mental state doesn't really count. You will be judged on your actions, and you must help yourself here because the world will be against you on this one. Where there has been a traffic accident with serious injuries, don't take a blood, breath or urine test if you can help it. Make the police get a search warrant to take evidence out of your body... and get an experienced lawyer who practices drunk driving law immediately.

O.K. Let's see if I got it straight so far. I can refuse a field sobriety test and the cop can't do anything about it, but if I refuse an alcohol test, they can suspend my license. Isn't that it?

Generally, that's right... but! The police may seize your blood alcohol content from your body in some circumstances. The United States Supreme Court has decided that a state's legislature has the ability to "force a driver to submit to a blood alcohol test without violating the driver's Fifth Amendment right against self incrimination," *South Dakota v. Neville*, 459 U.S., 103 S.Ct. 916, 918 (1983). They can do this without consent and without a warrant where:

1. The driver has already been arrested, usually for another offense (vehicular homicide);

2. The state's implied consent law permits it;

3. The driver's blood has been taken for another purpose (medical treatment).

This doesn't take into account where you simply run into a hard-ass cop who wants it all... your license, your career, your body in jail. Some states condone this approach but, thankfully, most cops are reasonable. If you had a major accident with serious injuries, any cop will chase you for an alcohol test. If it's just a routine traffic stop, the cop will usually let your refusal stand. It's got to be a slow night in the burg, when the cop really wants to jerk you around, because most police procedures say, under non-emergency, non-accident circumstances, the cop should honor your refusal of an alcohol test and just take your license.

And I repeat: Don't take a field sobriety test, ever. Remember the driver in our opening scenario? He was sober at the time of testing and still flunked. You have a free and unfettered right to refuse. If the cop is asking for a field sobriety test, he's now looking for the additional probable cause needed to demand a breath or blood test. Although, it's easier said than done, refuse him. It may take a little creativity, particularly when the cop says, "I said get outta the goddamn car, asshole, before I zap you on the nuts with my stun gun!" Cops have a way of being persistent, even when they know they are wrong. Tell him your hemorrhoids are bleeding real bad; he'll leave you alone.

A field sobriety test is a coordination test, not a sobriety test (make sense?) and state courts are not altogether convinced of the test's value. There are a zillion reasons, none of them related to alcohol, which explain why a test subject cannot count to ten, say the alphabet, walk a straight line, pick up coins or repeat "two all beef patties, special sauce, lettuce, cheese, pickles, onions, all on a sesame seed bun" backwards.

Field sobriety tests are also considered semi-scientific, but I think this reputation hops on one leg... the horizontal gaze nystagmus test. Given the exotic name and a cop's natural demand for state-of-the-art technology, this crime fighting tool is a disappointment. It's a pencil. You look at the pencil, the cop moves it slowly left to right and then back, looking for your eyes to quiver. Two quivering eyes and bingo, you're under arrest. As silly as this high-tech pencil test sounds, the U.S. Department of Transportation recognizes it as the most accurate indication of inebriation in the field test battery. Even those gimmicky, hand held preliminary breath testers that police departments have recently become so enamored with on your money are no match for pencil test accuracy. Courts universally have labeled the preliminary breath testers as junk, too inaccurate to give a true alcohol result. But the cops have a dilemma with a horizontal gaze nystagmus test as well. They usually can't get the test results into evidence without introducing an expert witness to explain and qualify the procedure. Want to know why your eyes quiver when you are drunk? So does the jury. Here it is. Horizontal gaze nystagmus is an involuntary jerking of the eyes as they move side to side. Alcohol exaggerates and magnifies the jerking movements. A drunk's brain gives stronger commands to the eyes to overcome alcohol's effects, coordination is reduced and the eyes move in distinct, obvious jerks.

It seems simple enough but a judge won't permit horizontal or lateral gaze nystagmus test results into evidence without first knowing what it all means, explained by someone who knows what they are talking about. Experts cost money and police departments have budgets. If a cop pulls a pencil on you, unless he is the expert, he's probably just playing with it. Still, don't give him any satisfaction. Don't take his test, don't look at his pencil. It's his case; make him prove it.

Why do I need to know this legal stuff? I just keep a little bottle under the seat. If I get stopped, I chug-a-lug when the cop approaches. The test won't be able to figure if I was drinking before or after I was driving, right?

Wrong. Bad idea, but it's a commonly held bad idea. Many people think you can beat the chemical test by drinking an alcoholic beverage when the cop appears. This tactic only guarantees that the driver will get taken in for a chemical test. As the fresh alcohol passes into the blood stream, it also insures a stronger blood alcohol content later. Alcohol in the blood follows a bell-curve: It rises, peaks and falls. You can always hire an expert forensic toxicologist to relate back the percentage of alcohol in the blood when the test was taken, but most of the case law runs against you. Courts have considered the relation-back (retrograde extrapolation) theory and found that:

1. Three to four hours is not too long a wait between the stop and the test;

2. A driver's actions and appearance at the time of the traffic stop can certify that the later taken test results are indeed accurate; and

3. In a lot of states, the relation-back theory is simply invalid by statute or order of court because they recognize the test results as per se drunk driving.

That shoots the booze bottle under the seat idea, and that's why you need to know more about this legal stuff or get someone on your side who does. The law can work both ways, and that brings us to the next question regarding attorneys. O.K., you in the back with the Fu Manchu 'stache.

Yeah, like, I know the guy who got my cousin, Vinnie, his divorce. Vinnie really got over. I'll bet this guy would be really good for a drunk driving charge, huh?

Maybe, but probably not. If the divorce lawyer never tried a drunk driving case, he's going to be pretty useless in a criminal courtroom. Even if you think this lawyer would be great in any kind of courtroom, I still suggest that you find a lawyer who regularly practices drunk driving law. He knows the cops, he knows the applicable law, he knows the judges, the secretaries, clerks, tipstaffs and bailiffs. He knows the system that you are trying to beat. It's an old lawyer's boast: "I don't have to know the law, I know the judge."

It's just better to have someone on your side who knows all the players. But if you insist on using a lawyer who doesn't practice drunk driving law, spring for about 150 bucks and buy this book: *DWI Defense Forms and Checklists*, by John A. Tarantino, James Publishing Group, P. O. Box 25202, Santa Ana, CA 92799, (714) 556-0960.

The competition isn't bad either: *Drunk Driving Defense,* Second Edition, by Lawrence Taylor, Little, Brown and Company, Boston and Toronto.

And: *Intoxication Test Evidence: Criminal and Civil,* by Edward F. Fitzgerald and David N. Hume, The Lawyers Co-operative Publishing Company, Rochester, New York 14694, Bancroft-Whitney Company, San Francisco, California 94107.

To my knowledge, there are no better road maps for a lawyer to plan his way through a drunk driving trial.

O.K. But if I want a lawyer who specializes in drunk driving cases, how do I find one?

Ask around in the right places. Bartenders, bar owners and regular patrons know the lawyers who practice drunk driving law. So do the court secretaries and court administrative personnel. All the cops know the players. If you can get the cop who arrested you to recommend a lawyer, you're probably on your way to getting your case fixed. In any case, when you go to your interview with a lawyer, ask him about his experience with drunk driving cases. It's your money.

Hey, wait a minute. Did you say I can get my case fixed?

It's been done. It's also very dangerous. You may be trading up for real jail time. We'll discuss this when we get to the questions on bribes.

Do you say I should offer the cop a bribe?

I guess I know what's important, so we'll cover the corruption issues now. No! You should not offer the cop a bribe. The cop doesn't know you well enough to take a bribe from you. Bribery in official matters is always a felony. Even if the cop wants to take your money (or whatever else you are trading), he can't trust you to keep your end of the deal. Besides, government prosecutors are forever out there employing shills to entrap bad cops. It's like this. Cops make a lot of legal money these days. They have pensions, insurance, medical, dental and eye care benefits, and they have families. A cop will never accept money from a stranger unless the cop is even dumber than he looks. And most cops won't take money, period. It's just not worth it.

And if you offer the cop a bribe at the scene, you are committing a bigger crime than the drunk driving offense. While it's been done with some success, more often than not, the bribe-try is ignored, but noted for the record. When prosecuted, the only real defense to bribery is a confession to the drunk driving charge. Since bribery requires a specific intent by the briber, you have to admit that you were too drunk to know what you were doing in order to get the bribery charge dismissed. It's an effective cop whipsaw trick. A cop will often charge bribery only to get a guilty plea to the drunk driving charge.

Still... there are a few cops who like gold chains, fast cars and slow brain waves, and they might even seek you out. Now it's legal to ask the cop (but wait until after you have been charged) if he knows a good lawyer. If he says no, you now have your answer. He's sticking with the law. If he gives you a name, or better yet, the lawyer's card (I'll tell you why in a minute), now you have to decide what kind of person you are.

The next question is on me: O.K. Let's say that you go to see the cop's lawyer, now what?

Well, you have to play games first. The lawyer has even more to lose than the cop. You are protected by the lawyer-client privilege if you later talk to investigators about a fix, but the lawyer can't legally keep *your* mouth shut. If you tell the lawyer up front that you were arrested by Officer X and that Officer X then suggested that you see him for representation, the lawyer will generally settle in and take over. Unless the lawyer is dumber than he looks, he will not discuss a fix or a bribe in explicit terms, but you will come away with a pretty good idea of what's going on, mostly because he didn't discuss your case very much, he didn't act very lawyer-like, and he quoted you a fee, up front, that knocked your socks off. If the lawyer says: "My fee is five thousand dollars, but if we don't win, I'll give back four thousand," you can fairly well expect that the lawyer is doing business with the cop and/or the D.A. and the judge. Lawyers don't give back money. But this corruption attempt is very dangerous. Prosecutors decimated the Chicago criminal court system over drunk driving cases a few years ago with Operation Greylord. Jail and suicide were common results. Be forewarned.

What's the next question? You over there with the tattoos and earrings.

Hey! If bribery is, like, illegal, man, how 'bout... oh... can I get my money back after my case gets dumped?

There is a way. If you are, like, that special kind of person who makes a deal with his fingers crossed and hidden behind the back, yes, you can get your money back, and maybe more; but you have to work for it. The cashier's line starts at any of three places: a newspaper, a prosecutor's office or the Federal

Bureau of Instigation. You go to the newspaper first and speak with the editors for a number of reasons:

1. They will do most of the work for you. Most newspapers, as well as radio and television stations, are owned by large corporations. You know, the people who own and run America. The F.B.I. routinely works as a private security/investigative police force for the large corporations. If Hearst or Gannett or Scripps' people make the call, the F.B.I. will jump. Don't believe me? Well, if a kid in your neighborhood disappears, the feds are charged with the investigation. After a day or so of bumbling around, they read the parents their rights, ask for a confession, then disappear themselves until the state or locals crack the case or find the kid. Then they reappear and announce with a media blitz that federal computers worked all night to save the day.

   Now, rob a bank and see what happens. Even if you only get peanuts, the federals will chase you until you die, and in some cases, beyond, if they haven't recovered The Man's money. Remember D.B. Cooper? Twenty years later, they are still chasing the money he parachuted with into the night from a sky-jacked 727. Two army battalions searched the great northwest woods for a week looking for Cooper and The Man's $250,000. It cost the taxpayers ten times what D.B. Cooper stole from the banks and insurance companies, all for the chase of a quarter million dollar ghost. When it's your money, money is no object, especially if the F.B.I. is spending it.

   So, what is important to the F.B.I. is protecting monied interests and basking under media limelights. They *will* jump when an editor calls with a corruption tip.

2. The second reason you go to the media is to keep everybody honest. Editors win awards for this kind of stuff, but they have to swim in the same water as everyone else. They will dog a story if there is something in it for them. Awards mean raises for writers and editors. A good corruption ex-

pose might finally get their salaries up to minimum wage. Why do you think the elitists thought Citizen Kane was such a good citizen? Because he didn't pay anybody.

3. The last reason for going to the papers first is self-protective. If the worm turns on you, you want a record or notice somewhere other than the police station that you were really *trying* to be civic before you got arrested for bribery and fell victim to a fatal accident at the police station. Did anyone ever tell you that if it ain't broke, don't fix it?

Just know who you are dealing with. Media people are parasitic bloodsuckers. They tell you that the people have a right to know, then charge the people half-a-buck a copy to exercise their right. They will sell you out, too. Remember, it's only money. Now the federals are special people as well. It's no secret in most districts that F.B.I. offices have too many agents and too little work. Half of their business seems to come from chasing bank tellers who counted The Man's money with super glue on their fingers. The feds desperately need real cases, high profile, corruption cases that show the world how busy and effective they are. They will spend a million of your tax dollars tracking, indicting and prosecuting just one little justice of the peace in Buckwheat County, Georgia for (allegedly) taking a fifty dollar bribe. It's good enough for government work, so long as it hits the papers.

But they screw things up more often than not. Here's a joke I stole from a cop novel (*The Friends of Eddie Coyle* by George V. Higgins): What are the three most over-rated things in America? Home cooking, home pussy and the F.B.I.

F.B.I., indeed. They tracked Al Capone for ten years, but it was the I.R.S. who put him away. It's usually the same with public corruption cases. F.B.I. agents bang through the neighborhood like a platoon of garbage men, making noise and getting attention, but in the end it's the I.R.S. bean-counters who bag the crooks. Even if your lawyer didn't give you a receipt for your five thousand dollars, the I.R.S. can not only prove that he got the money, but they can show within pennies what he did with it. Your finances tell what kind of guy you are and a good investigator will read your checkbook like a diary. If the lawyer has *any* secret (sex, drugs, gambling), even if he didn't do anything wrong, the I.R.S. will give him reasons to rat-fink on others. But it's the F.B.I. that provides the courtroom script. So once again, expect screw-ups.

The F.B.I. will investigate and prosecute corrupt cops, judges, lawyers and district attorneys until their noses bleed... if you make their case for them. And they will make any kind of deal to get it done, including giving your money back. But beware! The F.B.I. also makes deals with their fingers crossed and hidden behind their back. There are no bigger renegers in the land, especially if they blow the case... and they usually will, no matter how good your information, because they were trained to blow. The F.B.I. was founded by a fairy, remember. And if their case fails, expect to get tossed back to the state for re-charging of the up-until-recently-fixed drunk driving charge, and... get this, a new charge of conspiracy for bribery in criminal or official matters.

Even if the feds walk away from you, or even get you your money back, it doesn't mean that the state is so obliged. It would be wise to have your new lawyer, if you can get one, force the state prosecutors to sign off on your deal with the feds, up front, *before* the feds blow the case, the deal and anything else they find blowable.

Whoever said life was fair? State prosecutors are never too happy to see federal investigators swishing around in *their* neighborhoods. There is a natural tension and resentment here among competing predators. The feds have outrageous power and money (yours), which gives rise to well deserved jealousy. Further, they don't need any special authorization to track drunk driving corruption. They are simply tracking the flow of federal highway safety money from the Bundestag to the states, making sure that Uncle Sam gets a fair count. That is exactly why the F.B.I. sees enemies everywhere. This is the nineties. If you drive, you're a suspect. Happy motoring and watch your pee-pee.

What if I want to keep my case fixed, but the F.B.I. comes anyway; should I talk to them?

Not yet. You have every legal right to tell them to buzz off. Remember, God made laws and man made mirrors to reflect them, but what really works in this world are bribes and threats. Now that you have paid your bribe, it's possible that the F.B.I. will come threatening. But what they really want is to be your friend. They are not like the others. Uh-huh.

Tell the F.B.I. agents (they are like tits: they come in pairs) that you have a lawyer and you will talk through him. They are now prohibited under their own rules from violating your attorney-client privilege, and you don't even have to tell them who your lawyer is. They will bluster a while, but all they can really do now is come back and give you a grand jury subpoena. Guess what? You are getting one anyway, particularly if you tell them up front the incidents of your case. Once they leave, immediately go back to the lawyer who got your case fixed and tell him of your visit. *DON'T USE THE TELEPHONE!* If the investigation has gone this far, the lawyer's and possibly your own phone calls are being registered to see who is talking to whom. It is unlikely that they are being recorded, but... since we don't need to spend so much money fighting the Russians anymore, it's a good bet the excess cash went to law enforcement, and today's gadgets might not even violate the wiretap law. In one case, the feds fired a tiny dart with a mini amplifier into a lawyer's window pane, then picked the amplified sound waves off the window with a receptor. They heard every peep in the office, and it wasn't ruled an intrusion.

A typical F.B.I. trick is to get a grand jury authorization for a pen register on the target's telephone, then send the dogs out to scare the hell out of prospective witnesses. The pen register is a device that records the time and phone numbers of calls between the parties, and it doesn't require a warrant or court authorization. The feds can simply go to the phone company and do it. When the unsuspecting witness calls the target, in this case the fixing lawyer, the feds immediately know that patchwork has begun, so they crank up the heat and send the dogs back out to threaten the prospective witness. At this point, he has to think the F.B.I. lives in his house and his wife is an informant. He is ready to crack.

Now, if your lawyer blows you off, screw him, he had his chance. Go to another lawyer and let him deliver you to the feds *after* you have been granted immunity from prosecution.

But more probably, your fixing lawyer will step in to protect your mutual asses. He will get you a second lawyer, *free*, to coach and guide you through future grand jury proceedings. If the original deal was handled properly, with head shakes, uh-huhs and talking in tongues rather than explicit statements like, "I'm gonna bribe the freakin' judge. That'll be five big ones," then the whole mess will go away after about a year of serious harassment by your tax dollars at work. That is, if everybody keeps their mouths shut. If they don't, then as your lawyer, I advise you to dump, and dump on the chumps. Remember when I told you it was better if the cop gave you the lawyer's card, or at least wrote the name down for you. Put the card in a plastic bag immediately and hide it somewhere in case trouble comes. If the lawyer and/or the cop have set you adrift, you now have the one piece of evidence that will *prove* business was done between them.

The federals will forgive a crooked cop to nail a sleazy lawyer, and they will only lightly spank the lawyer if he rolls over on a corrupt judge. That card, with the cop's fingerprints or handwriting, puts the cop under hot lights. He now must explain to a grand jury why he wanted to help you and why he wanted to help *that* lawyer. It can't be done. Federal prosecutors routinely maneuver grand juries like cows in the pasture. When the herd is moving, indictments are inevitable. Save the card, look for the lawyer's help and stay quiet, meanwhile.

A noted gangster once told me, "Never tell your lawyer more than he can find out for himself." Silence is the by-word for everyone. One word and it's 'bye.

Well, if I get arrested for drunk driving, can I at least sue the bar?

Probably only if you wreck. Either a state's statutory Dram Shop Act or a common law negligence theory will get you into court if you wreck, especially if the crash was your fault. As for getting arrested, courts still look at this as your own fault. No one made you drink it, right? It's your consumption rather than the bartender's service that got you into the jackpot.

What if I've been drinking and I wreck, what should I do?

Everybody come up to the front of the room on this one. It's the most important question in the book. I'm going to speak low because the information is... *secret.* And I can keep a secret, it's the people I tell who can't.

Over 20,000 people a year die from alcohol-related accidents across the United States. Usually, the drunk driver is among the dead. So much for the common misconception that drunks roll with the punch. But many more accidents are minor. This is where the cops make their arrests. A good guess is that about half of the drunk driving arrests nationwide rise from vehicle accidents, most of them one car run-offs or fender benders.

Most drunk drivers I see in court got arrested waiting for someone to come along and help them get their car back on the road or give them a ride home.

When a cop is dispatched to a traffic accident, he is already thinking "drunk driver." If you have been drinking and then wreck, when the cop comes along, the probable cause for arrest is automatic. The odds are overwhelming that you will be charged with drunk driving.

What if you are not there?

Well, it's illegal in all states to hit and run.

But, let's distinguish first between a hit and run driver and one who just left the scene of an accident. A hit and run driver is a bad guy. From the moment of the crash, he is trying to escape. He has no concern for who or what he hit. He doesn't care about injuries to others or damage to property. His goal is to escape, an anonymous maniac who, unrepentant, races away from criminal liability that may include murder if he is apprehended. Courts and juries have no sympathy for him. The driver's choice may be easy, but the chance is a double risk. And police officers take hit and run drivers personal. The better advice, and the law, is to stop at the scene of an accident that involves you.

A driver is charged with a duty to stop, check for injuries, render aid and assistance to victims and identify himself. In circumstances of serious injury, I advise that this is the only course of conduct, but don't, under any circumstances that you can control, let the cop take you for a chemical test. Don't give evidence against yourself; you may be consenting to a murder charge.

At an accident without injuries, a driver is generally permitted to leave the scene after he has identified himself or left notice for the absent, damaged property owner. Cops don't, and don't have to, investigate all traffic accidents. A run-in with a tree, guide rail or telephone pole is not necessarily reportable. For a single vehicle accident, with no injuries, your choice is fairly clear. Put a notice on the property you whacked, if the property was personal to someone (a building or shed), then get the hell out before some volunteer comes along and screams "Call a cop!" Some property, like trees and big rocks, doesn't call for any notice at all; and things like telephone poles, highway rails, light stands or the World War I doughboy in Central Park are better taken care of tomorrow by your insurance agent. If you go to the police station a day later, sober, and fess up to knocking the lantern off someone's front yard statue of a little black boy greeter, you are not going to get spanked very hard and certainly not for drunk driving. Besides, that's why you buy automobile insurance. *Nationwide* expects you to wreck sometime. Let your insurance agent handle it; that's what you pay him for. Don't wait around at an insignificant wreck and ask the cop to arrest you. That's pushing good citizenship to a bad fault.

Police who find a wrecked or abandoned vehicle off the highway usually think that the driver left to get help. It's not illegal. While they may think that the driver was drunk, they relax a little when their investigation shows an absence of blood trails or other indications of injury. Still, they will look for you because there may have been injuries, and it's a job put on them that they can't avoid.

There are no hard rules in this circumstance, but the big laws on privacy work in your favor. With this in mind, here's a suggested checklist if you wreck:

1. Check immediately for injuries to yourself, passengers, pedestrians or people in other vehicles. If there are any injuries to persons other than yourself, serious law obliges you to stick around and care for the injured until adequate help arrives. This means cops and ambulances.

2. If there are no injuries, your next obligation is to give notice of your name, address and phone number either to another driver or by placing the written information on an unattended vehicle. Remember that cops don't necessarily need to be involved at every accident scene, but you should, and in some states must, advise them of your accident. "Tomorrow" is the best day to do that. But don't tell the police that your car was stolen. They didn't believe the last three guys today who wrecked, then reported stolen vehicles. They won't believe you either. And they will be pissed enough that they will demand a face to face interview. Even if they can't charge drunk driving, they will look at charging you for false reports. Play it straight: "I wrecked last night, nobody hurt, just thought you guys would like to know. Bye."

3. If your car is driveable, you should get it off the road to the nearest safe spot where another drunk driver won't slam into it. You should not drive it home or any other long distance because: (a) You have already proved that you are too drunk to drive by crashing; and (b) The cops are probably already responding to your accident, and they will see you driving as they approach.

Many drunk driving charges are dismissed because the cop cannot place the driver behind the wheel, so don't be there. After you wreck, safely secure your vehicle and get away from it. If the damage was very minor and the accident was not your fault, let's say you got hit by another drunk driver much more under the influence than you, then maybe you are sober enough to drive to a safe place, away from the accident where the cops can't easily hunt you up. It's your call. You were driving drunk in the first place. How far do you want to push your luck?

4. If your vehicle is not driveable, get help; get a tow truck, get a horse, but get it off the road... quickly. Leave the warning flashers on if they still work. Set up any other warning devices you may have down the road and along the berm. The

cop who finds your vehicle will be impressed with your concern for safety. No way could you be drunk. Do not return to the scene, period. Drunk drivers have been arrested and convicted after being taken out of the tow truck or found walking around the accident scene hours after the crash. Judges and jurors aren't as dumb as they look. They can see that it was your car. What the hell were you doing around it several hours after the wreck? Even when a jury only wants to convict you of "dumb," it still goes into your record as "drunk." When you are gone, stay gone.

5. Okay, here it is. Where do you go after the crash? If the cops found your car wrecked along the highway, they just have to satisfy their curiosity so they will come looking. As your lawyer, I advise you not to go home. It's the first place cops look after they call in your license plate information. Go to a friend's house, go to a motel, go to church (they will never look for you there). Like in a game of tag, these are generally "safe bases." A very unsafe base is the nearest saloon because it's a very likely place for the cops to look, and they don't need an arrest warrant to snatch you out of the bar. It's a public place, and the cops can remove you, unchallenged, for so many reasons that you practically have no privacy interest whatsoever when they come looking. The idea that you can drink more alcohol *after* the accident and confuse the issue whether you were drunk while driving versus drunk after driving is workable, but it's best put to work at a safe base where the cops can't get at you without first getting an arrest warrant. Ironically, home, the place you should not go because the cops are certainly coming there, is actually your safest base... if you follow the rules that I now give you. Here's the legal stuff:

In *Welsh v. Wisconsin,* 466 U.S. 740, 104 S. Ct. 2091, 80 L.Ed. 2d 732 (1984), the cops chased and arrested Welsh in his own house after he ran his car off the road and into a field. The United States Supreme Court ruled that Welsh's arrest and conviction for drunk driving was invalid because the cops didn't first get an arrest warrant to snatch Welsh out of his home. The court reasoned that drunk driving was not a serious enough offense to overcome Welsh's right of privacy in his own home. But remember early on that I told you laws are not absolute? Chief Justice Rehnquist disagreed on this case and he's calling the shots now on the Supreme Court. This was a 1984 case; drunk driving laws have since been strengthened across the country. While this case is still good law now, I'd think about voting Democrat for a couple years to keep it that way. It's a Nixon-Reagan-Bush Supreme Court. Don't blame that trusting, simple-minded peanut picker when your own lights go out.

A little older case, *Payton v. New York*, 445 U.S. 573, 100 S. Ct. 1371, 63 L. Ed. 2d 639 (1980), held that a warrantless arrest or search for suspects under far more important circumstances, homicide and drugs, was still invalid because no warrant had been issued. This case flatly says "no warrant, no entry" under anything but the most dire conditions. Of course, Justice Rehnquist dissented on this one as well, under the idea that a suspect could just surrender at his front door thereby not subjecting himself to an illegal, warrantless roust within his house. Right. And we promises not to whup you either, boy.

But *Welsh* and *Payton* still guide your fourth amendment right of protection against an arrest in your home without a warrant, and the cops probably won't have a warrant unless someone is dying or dead. In that case, refer back to my earlier advice about doing the right thing. So the short order is, if you make it inside your home, stay inside, even if the cops yell "fire." They cannot come into your house, or your friend's house, or your motel room without an arrest warrant based on probable cause that a felony has been committed, and almost all drunk driving charges are misdemeanors with mail process by summons. Even if you get collared on the spot, the cops often will paper you later with a complaint by mail. But churches, like barrooms, are open to the public so an arrest warrant isn't required to pull you out of church, but... if you were a cop, how would you feel about pulling a warrantless raid on the house of God?

The trick then is to get home and stay behind the door. Now, as your lawyer, I advise you to start drinking heavily. When the cop comes, greet him with a drink in your hand, offer him one, ask him inside but *don't* answer his questions. You're lawfully drunk, in the sanctity of your own home, so mumble, mush your way through the conversation, and *don't* step outside your house. Most cops know that you are safe on base so they will ask you outside to your porch, steps or lawn so that they may lawfully arrest you. If they can get you outside, they will claim that you consented to arrest, and they will win. Remember, Chief Justice Rehnquist encourages citizen consent to police requests, so expect consent cases to be a big part of Supreme Court law for the next ten years. Today's cops always ask you to consent whenever they cannot lawfully do what they want. So when a cop asks you to consent to a search, an interview, custody or arrest, ask him what will happen if you don't. If his answer is anything more than "I'll hit you upside your !?*! head," he wouldn't be asking for consent in the first place. Cops may be often wrong but when they are right, God has to reverse their legal authority because the Supreme Court won't. And God has recused Him/Her/Itself on decision-making votes for the past 5000 years.

Here is an illustration of your best course of conduct after getting into your house. I remember a particularly bad "B" movie from my little kid days of hiding under the front seats at the Saturday monster matinee, *Attack of the Robot People*, I think it was. A man was chased along the street and back to his apartment by a clanking killer robot. He warned his inquiring wife several times, "Don't open the door, Martha!" Supercilious to the end, she opened the door and came face to face with the killer robot whereupon her husband said, "I told you not to open that door, Martha."

So don't open the door. Hide. Sleep. Lock and bar the windows and doors. If the cops come in with a warrant later, you can pretty well figure that you're in deep shit because they usually won't come busting in with an arrest warrant unless someone is dead or dying.

My lawyer is the laziest man on earth, but he's my brother-in-law, so he comes cheap. He says if I ever get arrested for drunk driving, I should just waive the charges to court and plead guilty. I won't get punished very hard. Is he right?

If you rely on his advice, I would do two things afterward: Sue him for malpractice and get a divorce lawyer for when your wife sides with her brother. *Never* waive drunk driving charges to court! Most states have screening, pre-trial or preliminary hearings where a magistrate or municipal court judge decides the worthiness of a drunk driving charge before trial. This is not only your best chance to beat the charge, this is where you catch cops lying and where you make a record so they can't lie again at trial. Pre-trial hearings are like exhibition games before the big match that counts. Usually, both sides get to feel each other out, learn something about their opponent's case and then tailor their strategy *and testimony* for trial. But the best thing about these kinds of hearings for you is that you don't have to present a defense, but the prosecutor has to lay out his case. That means you hear what the cops and witnesses have to say before trial, and they learn nothing about you. If you waive your case to court, you not only lose this edge, you give the cop an unchallenged opportunity to lie. While a cop can usually only make a misdemeanor arrest on view, he can arrest you after investigation for drunk driving if he has credible witnesses. When he only has to produce his witnesses once, at trial, he can have them coached to testify so that you practically can't refute them. In other words, he can make them say whatever he wants. At best, you get into a truth contest with the witnesses. That's like punching at someone who isn't in the fight. In that circumstance, it's not likely that a jury will be very sympathetic to your defense.

Here is a more vivid illustration of what I mean. Let's say a cop goes to a drunk driver's home and arrests him in his house without a warrant. We know that's illegal. But when the District Attorney informs the cop that his arrest was illegal and the case will be dismissed, what is the cop going to say? "Oh no, I arrested him on his front lawn. The guy was out of the house, he consented." Right. And because the driver waived his pre-trial hearing, he lost his chance to pin the cop down before trial. It's the cop's word against the driver's word now, and it's too late to determine the liar. Cops always win truth contests... unless you *prove* they are lying.

Now here's an example where you can sandbag the cop. Let's say you go to the pre-trial hearing, even without a lawyer, and you listen to the cop testify: "His car swerved over the center line four times so I pulled him over. He had a strong odor of alcoholic beverage about him, glazed eyes, flushed face and disheveled clothes. I gave him a field sobriety test and he failed all parts. On the one leg stand, he swayed four to six inches and had to steady himself on the car. Touching his nose he missed by an inch and a half with both fingers. When he said the alphabet he stuttered on G and he stopped and couldn't remember what came after L."

At this point, you think, "what the f-f-f...?" You know the cop is inventing things. You weren't so drunk that you couldn't remember what you did and didn't do. The cop is reading a script on you. There are no creatures of habit more addicted to routine than cops. Just the way they file charges or write reports tells a story on them. A cop who regularly files the same battery of charges — disorderly conduct, attempted assault on a police officer and resisting arrest — is telling you that he likes to beat on people for almost no reason. The defendant charged with the disorderly conduct here is more probably a victim of police brutality. A traffic cop who is always filing drug charges is telling you that he is a snoop who will ransack your car. A narcotics officer whose reports always show that he confiscated a couple grams of cocaine is keeping the stuff he grabs in larger busts.

So if the testimony sounds like a script, that's because it is a script. Cops read them all the time. I've heard a zillion cops, all bored to tears, recite the same lines from their reports, time after time in different drunk driving cases. There are two reasons for this. The first is that cops are too busy to take notes at the traffic stop so they rely on memory when they write their reports later at the station... and memory fails. The second reason is that no one ever challenges the report so it's easy to get away with the same symptoms of field sobriety test failure in case after case for different defendants. But if you go to the pre-trial hearing and listen to the cop testify from his report about things you know you didn't do, you have an excellent chance of refuting the cop and getting your case dismissed at trial.

All you have to do is pull several police reports from his last and next few previous drunk driving arrests. The reports are public records, any newspaper parasite will tell you that, and you are entitled to them.

If the cop invents test results in your case, he probably followed his own tried and proven script in the others. When you remember that a field sobriety test comprises a battery of events that require many mathematical and analytical observations by the cop, and he didn't write them down at the time, you know that the cop will often go with what worked for him before. But every driver doesn't sway four to six inches on the one leg stand, miss his nose by one and a half inches with both fingers and stutter at G then stop at L on the alphabet test. Expose the cop as reading a script in court, using the cop's own reports, and your case won't even make it to the jury. You're innocent.

But if you waived your rights to a pre-trial hearing, you will never know that the cop is going to read a script on you until the trial and then it's too late. If you have an experienced drunk driving lawyer, not your brother-in-law, he may discover the reports independently, but then *he* takes the credit for discovering the big lie and charges accordingly.

Finally, if you waive the pre-trial hearing, you may be missing a chance to settle your case without a conviction. Just as our nation's jails and criminal courtrooms are clogged with drunk drivers, our municipal, lower level courts and justices of the peace courts have the same heavy caseloads. But because of the informal nature of these initial courts, police and prosecutors are more willing to negotiate and reduce a drunk driving charge to plain or public drunkenness, which only carries a fine, since they are in the early stages of prosecution. Once a drunk driver has gone up and into the court system, however, the tendency is to leave the case alone. That means any deal offers are shuffled through a lot more hands and any hand can break the deal. At the lower level, at most, it's only you, your lawyer, the magistrate, the cop and maybe the District Attorney's representative.

The important thing to know about pre-trial hearings is that the cop has more control. It's still his case, not the system's... yet. And the cop may want to work a reduced plea unless he is a bounty hunter. A bounty hunter cop is in it for the money. He necessarily has to run the drunk driver to the very end of the line so that he can wring the last few pennies out of the system. But a reasonable cop just wants to do a job and it might be okay if the job ends with a fine by the magistrate. There are good reasons for this. First, the fine money for a reduced plea, say a drunk in public charge, usually goes to the municipality rather than the county or state system. As well, the cop is released from the hassle of trial court preparation, testimony and inconvenience. Every day a cop is in court is one less day the cop is on the street, or better, on vacation. That's two good reasons why municipal court dockets are choked with citations for public drunkenness instead of complaints for drunk driving. One thing a cop knows is how to do his own job.

But too many reduced charges in one courtroom can bring trouble or at least trouble-makers. Certainly representatives from the anti-drunk driving groups will come along to demand the death penalty, and often they are trailed along by their good buddies from (where else?) the F.B.I. The F.B.I. believes that money has always changed hands; no one ever borrows their neighbor's lawn mower and Santa Claus is a fiction created by Jewish merchants. Favors only exist in the minds of people who sell them.

But a cop *will* cut you a break. I've seen it, often. Sometimes, particularly if they are older cops, they will lock your car and take you home, no charge. They might otherwise take you into the station, then only file a disorderly conduct or public drunk citation against you. And they will lower a drunk driving charge sometimes at the preliminary hearing. Did your mother ever tell you that well-dressed people always wear underwear and a smile? She was right. A good attitude can soften the ego of even a hard-ass cop. Drunk drivers can be likable creatures. It's up to them.

What you're really telling me is to bend over and kiss the cop's ass, right?

I'm telling you to do whatever works. If there is a chance that being pleasant and civil is going to keep you out of a jackpot, why worry about your *own* ego? I've heard cops testify many times that a guy talked himself into trouble. What started as a warning becomes an official police crusade to wallop the ass-hole. Whispers go through the network to other cops and into judges' chambers, "This guy is a jerk."

If you call a cop "sir," "ma'am" or "officer," act sensible and decent, what you are really doing is acting sober. But there are some pretty specific *don'ts* involved here.

A drunk driving stop is not at all like a traffic stop. At a pure traffic stop, you talk. While excess chatter is an indication of inebriation, when you haven't been drinking, it's recommendable that you try to talk yourself out of trouble at a traffic stop: "Officer you caught me fair and square. I know I was doing 103 miles an hour back there, but I have diarrhea, my wife's in labor, the kid has a little league game, my dog just died and my accelerator stuck. I must have got excited. The radio just said Bush re-bombed Baghdad."

At a routine traffic stop, you want to keep the cop engaged until he either lets you go or burns you off with a ticket. *But,* when you have been drinking, shut up. Still, be nice about it. The trick here is to make the cop think (1) you're not that drunk; (2) you're a nice guy; and (3) you deserve a break today. But if he asks you to take a field sobriety test, you're already past the first stage, so be nice, but refuse.

It's not necessary that you suck up to the cop, but little gestures of polite conduct, smiles and agreeable nods, go a long way toward establishing that you are a human being and not an asshole.

There is one word of caution. Never agree with the cop's assessment that you are drunk. That has to be scientifically proved unless you admit to it. It's alright to disagree in civil conversation. Congressmen use the mother-tongue against each other at every session and the congressional hall floors are filled with sugar at day's end.

I'm not worried about myself, I'm a careful driver even drunk. I'm afraid of the other drunk. How can I avoid him?

It has often occurred that a reasonably prudent drunk driver who did nothing wrong got arrested because a maniac drunk slammed into him. Accidents happen, even to sober people. The trick here is to highlight that the other guy is a classic drunk.

Throw all the attention his way and disappear as soon as possible. Take control of the situation until the cops come. Get both cars off the road, check for injuries, summon aid. Now get something in your mouth to disguise odor: chewing gum, mints, candy, cigarettes if you have to, and have your cards ready. When the cops arrive, point at the other driver and shout, "He's drunk!"

While the cop is distracted, slip him your cards. Now, Houdini, get the hell out of there. Unless someone is seriously injured and medical personnel haven't arrived yet, you have pretty much complied with the legal requirements. You can always explain away tomorrow what the cop won't excuse today.

Cops are fairly sinister characters. They love to brag: "Shee-it! They was both drunk, so I double-banged 'em." And drunk driving convictions don't differentiate between "barely drunk" and "stinkin, shit-faced, falling down, fouled-up drunk" either. To a cop, drunk is drunk, and if you wait around, he will get to you eventually.

Maniac drunks are the bad guys. They are often repeat offenders, driving under a suspended license, reckless as hell and, according to the National Highway Traffic and Safety Administration, responsible for about 20,000 of this nation's annual 50,000 highway dead. They are 25 times more likely to kill than a normal driver. Ironically, they drive the big cars.

As the manufacturers down-sized and shifted to plastic during the 1980s in desperate attempts to meet the federal fuel efficiency standards, less steel meant less strength in the later vehicles. The hand-me-down "bulk cruisers" were passed on to the dirtbags, their ranks heavily populated with hard drinkers. Yuppies found to their acute dismay that a 1990 BMW was a solid underdog to an '81 Caddy. Even rusted, the big car usually scored a first-round knockout.

Here's a war story.

Not long ago, two fellows who ran a proctology clinic came before me as prosecution witnesses and victims of a maniac drunk driver. The facts showed that one morning about 7:00 a.m. as they were gayly heading for work in a small foreign sportster, humming along with the drive-time deejay (Lookin' for love in all the wrong places), they were violently rear-ended at a stop light by a suspended/recidivist/.31 drunk driver in a '73 Bonneville. Both of their pelvises were broken and their medical practice was unplugged for six months. But after the trial, I watched them leave the courthouse and climb into a huge Chevy Suburban.

If you want protection from the maniacs, take a lesson from the good doctors: leave the plastic at home and get a big truck, with a big engine, heavy-duty chassis, specially-made steel bumpers, and tail fins. It's a jungle out there and the natives are restless. They've been partying all night at the neighbor's rent party. Now they are ready for some serious drinking... and driving. America! What a country.

I drink a little but only to be social. What I do best is cocaine. Do I have anything to worry about if I get stopped?

A charge of driving under the influence of drugs is addressed in most states on an AND/OR basis. The criminal complaints are usually pre-printed with a little box for the computer/typist to check indicating "... driving, operating or controlling a vehicle on a state highway or trafficway ☐ while under the influence of alcohol; or ☐ a controlled substance; or ☐ under the combined influence of alcohol and a controlled substance . . ."

This leaves the police free to charge up front and sort things out later. The simple fact, however, is that driving under the influence of drugs is a tough charge to make and tougher to make stick. Traffic cops just don't know a lot about drugged driving. The experts admit that they need to learn a lot more about how different drugs, even legal ones, affect driving and motor skills. And most cops just can't tell if someone is on drugs. Because drugs are usually taken in association with alcohol, the effects can be masked so that a cop cannot recognize drug symptoms even if he has training in drug recognition behavior, and most traffic cops don't. As well, drugs may leave no common trademark behavior and often may affect different people in different ways.

There are some easy guesses, of course, and some tough ones. While a wild-eyed hippie with reefer-breath and "Oh Wow, man!" exclamations every five seconds is pretty easily targeted for marihuana, a yuppie with a cocaine-face can often be undetectable. What makes one man giggle makes another gasp with an exploded heart. Add the galaxy of uppers, downers, reds, greens, screamers, laughers (ether), buzzers, amyls, hunter pills and pineal glands and a chemical test can be one big pinwheel spin through the periodic elements chart. And the diagnosis can be all wrong. A urine test hours after eating a poppy seed bagel can show positive results for heroin. Rub a little Vicks VapoRub under your nose and a later pee test can pin amphetamines on you. Meanwhile, the stuff can stick around forever. A blood test weeks, sometimes months after ingesting drugs can show traces of marihuana or cocaine.

Since there is no *per se* statute for drugs, you don't need to show, as in the case of alcohol, a certain percent of drugs in the system. For driving under the influence of controlled substances, any dab will do ya. A trace of last Sunday's pot roach in the blood system can convict you of today's drugged driving even if you've been clean for a week. Prosecutors have been proficient at jailing drug runners, sellers and users, but the legal territory for drugged drivers is mostly Indian country. Everybody shoots first and asks questions later.

But four out of five times you can beat the cops.

It may be frightening when two cops stand alongside your car at a traffic stop and the younger one, while slapping a club into his glove, raises his suspicions: "I think he's on drugs, Sarge. Do you think he's on drugs? I'll bet he's on drugs. Look at his eyes, he must be on drugs. Can I beat the shit out of him?"

You know the rookie is right. What do you do? Simple; take a breath test *only*. Breath machines are manufactured specifically for alcohol detection, so the drugs won't show. If you haven't been drinking, the worst you are going to get is a dirty look from the rookie as you smirk on your way out. If you have been drinking, you may face a drunk driving charge, but you have ducked the drug offense which can carry multiple penalties for possession and make you a real criminal.

If you have any recent (give it a week anyway) drugs in your blood system, *DO NOT TAKE A BLOOD OR URINE TEST*.

The cops can have your blood and urine screened for drugs as well as alcohol, but they can't touch your breath. Since 80 percent of the chemical testing for alcohol done in the United States is by breath machine, all you need to do is go along with the cop's wishes. But get your consent to a breath test voiced way up front before the cop's suspicions of drug abuse arise. If you are asked to take a blood or urine test, fidget, fudge and fake your way out of it. Tell the cop you are a hemophiliac and can't take a blood test, you may bleed to death, then quickly consent to a breath sample. Almost nobody uses urine tests for alcohol anymore, so if you are requested to pee, the cop is either drug-conscious or a pervert. Tell him you have bladder problems and that your diaper is already messy; even an anxious pecker-checker would rather smell your breath in this instance.

If you do drugs, don't do a blood or urine test... And leave the driving to us.

I'm not concerned with most of what you're saying. All I care about is my driver's license, and I can get a special one for work if I get arrested, so I think you are full of B. S.

B. S. stands for big secrets, and I have one for you. Restricted driver's licenses for work use only are available in all but a few states, but these licenses are specifically prohibited for drunk drivers and other major violators. More commonly known as a "Bread and Butter" license, these licenses are issued for drivers whose regular licenses were suspended as a result of point accumulations from speeding, careless driving or routine roadway violations. If you were convicted of drunk or drugged driving, passing a flashing school bus or reckless driving in a school zone, you are not eligible for a "Bread and Butter" license. And if you recklessly drive past a flashing school bus while you are drunk, you'll get a meat and potatoes permit. You'll be meetin' the potatoes in the jailhouse kitchen. Ha! Take that, wise guy. Next question. The little fellow with the plaid bow tie in the second row.

Uh. Is there any way to keep my name out of the newspapers?

Well, it's possible, Pee-Wee, but remember who you are dealing with, huh? Journalists eat their own dead. When sports reporter Lisa Olsen had a face to face interview with a couple professional trouser-snakes, the news stories were slanted to make her look like a snake charmer. Granted she may be a journalist, but, what the hell, God forgives all sinners, right? She got foul fingered in her own paper after a feeble attempt to protect her failed, and a competing paper put the torch to her. Journalists eat everybody, and they do it for money. That means they can be bought off as well.

There are three places where you can kill a horror story before the beast savages your good name: the police station, the courthouse and the reporter *itself*. A reporter will do a little business now and then, but only when there is no competition and no risk. In a one-horse town, a reporter may overlook a news item for the proper stimulus, a bribe or threat, because the reporter knows he is the only one looking. In a two-horse town, with another newspaper, radio or television station, the additional scrutiny means you have to avoid the journalists altogether; and that is not a bad idea anyway, at least generally. In my judicial career, I have usually reserved only two comments for the media monsters: "No comment" and "Kiss my ass."

The rule is: If you can't fix the story, don't create a bigger one.

The better place to hide the ink is the police station, and that is where your lawyer gets involved. An experienced drunk driving lawyer knows all the cops by name, has made numerous trade-offs with them over the years and can ask for a favor: "Sarge, if my guy's name hits the papers, he'll take the bridge. When the snoops call in the morning, how about forgetting this one? I'll talk to the Chief and make sure there is no trouble."

For a drunk driving case, a cop doesn't care whether the story is printed or not. His job is prosecuting, not publicizing, so it's no big deal. Cops are truly reasonable when it comes to hiding a story, especially if they know the drunk driver is going to plead guilty and go quietly into the night. And cops don't like reporters either. The pencil is mightier than the sword. Cops often get lead poisoning themselves from the newsroom nebshits. But have your lawyer get to them immediately. Police reports go through a lot of channels. Too many hours and too many hands make it inevitable that one of the channels will be on television.

If you have not succeeded with the police, the final place to kill a story is the courthouse, and it's the easiest. Most state court judges, magistrates and justices are elected. They are politicians at least once during their careers, so journalists are their natural enemies. If the reporter does not know that the charges exist, there is an excellent chance that your case can be run on the secret docket. Courts are very system-oriented; it goes something like this: Assault cases on Monday, felony trials always start on Tuesday, drunk driving sentences go in a mob on Friday. Your lawyer can usually put you in front of a judge on a day when no one is looking, quickly cut a deal with the district attorney for a year's probation, $500 in fines and costs and a little community service; and you are gone in a half-hour with no publicity.

Take it from me, judges are even more reasonable than cops on this issue. We don't like the F.B.I., but we hate reporters. Investigators need cause to harass and intimidate; reporters need nothing because they have the First Amendment which is freedom of speech. But it means freedom of their speech, not yours, since the information corporations *own* the First Amendment, and the First Amendment owns the U.S. Constitution. Where a cop needs a search warrant to invade your privacy, a reporter only needs his title. Don't cooperate with them and don't talk to them unless it's in your own interest. Remember, you are dealing with people who eat dead cats.

I'm a sensible driver, but I have a couple drinks on my way home sometimes. These bounty-hunter cops scare me. Do you have any tips on how to avoid them?

The whole idea here is to know when you can prudently drive after you have been drinking. Alcohol is a depressant, even a little in the bloodstream will slow down your reaction time and attention span. It makes you an easy prey at the sudden leap of the bounty hunter. It is important then that you don't attract attention. Attention attracts the predator.

There are some obvious steps you should first take to protect yourself. When you come out of the barroom, check your car immediately for chalk marks on the tires. A bounty-hunter cop will often chalk the tires of every car in a tavern parking lot so that he can keep track of how long someone has been in the bar. He'll hit the right rear tire with slash marks, one mark at 3 o'clock, another mark at 5 o'clock, a third mark at 7 o'clock. You get the idea. Four marks, and the target has put in an eight hour shift bellied-up to the bar. If your car has any chalk marks and you have been drinking, DON'T DRIVE! You are being watched, and you *will* get stopped as soon as you pull onto the road.

Examine your vehicle carefully. The bounty-hunter cop makes his living arresting drunk drivers, and he doesn't play fair. He will *give* you a flickering taillight by bashing a hole through the plastic cover so that he has probable cause to stop you an hour from now. He will distract you with unassuming questions (Do you live very far from here, how many miles you figure?) so that you can't fully concentrate on locating your cards or performing a field sobriety test. He will lie to you ("Just tell me the truth, buddy, how long you been drinkin'? I'm not gonna charge you.") then use your admission against you in court. And even though he's in it for the money, you can't bribe him. A cop can make several hundred dollars in overtime and court and witness fees on one drunk driver, with much of the money tax-free. While one drunk driving arrest a week makes the cop an honorable reputation as a crusader, it also makes him an extra ten to fifteen thousand dollars a year. He gets the cash plus public acclaim, so the bounty hunter doesn't have to play fair.

Still, there are a few things you can do to protect yourself. Look at your car *before* you start drinking. Do your lights all work? Is your license plate current and clearly displayed? A bounty hunter can stop you for dirt obstructions on the plate; and I know one piggie who carries his own mud-mix that he smears on while the driver is in the bar. Check your car, lights, tires and plate before and after you drink. Finally, do you have valid inspection, emission and residency stickers in place? I have seen many drivers who got pulled over only because they were not current with a five dollar sticker, got smelled-up by the cop, then got arrested for drunk driving. Shame on them. They traded a couple dollar violation for a criminal offense.

You can't give the bounty-hunter cop an edge. He's got the law on his side and you in his sights. He will invent the probable cause needed to stop you. If you attract attention, he will arrest you.

So, when you leave the bar, stand outside and watch for a few minutes before you walk to your car. Look for the cop car. Try to park somewhere unnoticeable going in, behind the bar or in a nearby lot or down the road. When you drive away, go carefully but quickly into traffic, then drive with normal, prudent speed. Don't rush, even if you are late for an appointment. You aren't, all bar clocks are set ten minutes fast. Bartenders like to go home too.

If a cop pulls behind you right after you leave the bar, turn off the road immediately, *before* he has a chance to stop you. Pull into a parking lot, a 7-Eleven, a private driveway. Visit the stranger, but make the shark go back after another fish. He will. If a bounty hunter thinks there is any chance that you are sober, he will leave you alone. He needs production and there is nothing worse for him than a wasted chemical test. Too many stops with legal blood alcohol results and the cop gets beat up in court. His credibility fails.. and he doesn't get paid.

There are too many real drunk drivers out there. If you make the cop think that he is wasting his time, he'll go back to the feeding grounds. Remember: Big fish eat little fish, but camouflaged fish eat dinner at home. Don't attract attention, you will get there. How about a question from the Harley biker in the back row. Nice helmet, is that an S. S. original?

Uh, I dunno. I got it at a flea market... and I ride a Schwinn, but I'm a member of D.A.M.M., that's drunks against mad mothers. Wanna join?

No thanks, but it opens the door for me to make a couple statements about special interest groups. In America, it seems that there is nothing so good as a good idea. Everyone goes out to steal it. The early anti-drunk driving groups had good ideas. Make the public aware of the danger posed by drunk drivers and get them off the road. But it didn't take long for a proper-hearted volunteer group like M.A.D.D. to become big business, with millions in the bank and a big payroll of paid employees. Necessarily then, as a corporation with one message, the message had to grow stronger in order to continue perpetuating itself and the money it brought in. That means going after the small fry and marginal drunk drivers, encouraging prohibition and advocating ten years in the electric chair for first-time offenders, even as the advocate corporation took contributions from the big guys who make the stuff.

Don't drink and drive. Think before you drink. Know when to say when. We've become a nation of simplistic sloganeers. But who gets punished as a result of the propaganda? Not the maniacs, they are always in the line of fire anyway. The new net takes in all the fish. It's plain hypocritical, and with the *per se* standard, unfair. As the advocates' voices and wallets grew stronger, more and more state legislatures fell to their lobbying efforts and adopted the *per se* idea of drunk driving. It means smply that if you were driving and your blood alcohol content is above the state's statutory limit, say a .10 (that is one-tenth of one percent of total volume), then you are presumed guilty and that's that. Amazing. For every other crime in America, a person is presumed innocent. Drunk drivers fall into the sole exception, created by simple mathematics.

But does alcohol affect everyone in the same way? Take two healthy one hundred eighty pound men. One is groggy and out on four beers, the other, hours later, is like the Energizer bunny, still going. Only in Kentucky, where intoxication must be medically proved, is the system reasonably fair for everyone, even though Kentucky still has a "presumed" guilty level of intoxication. In every other state, even those few that have rejected the *per se* standard, you take your chances, not knowing if the last drink or the next one is going to put you over that invisible line called drunk driving.

I regularly see representatives of M.A.D.D., R.I.D., S.A.D.D. and a few of the newer anti-drunk driving groups in my courtroom. It's a free country, they are allowed. But in a jury trial, it's deadly to the defendant when a dozen paid "observers" pony into the courtroom, red ribbons streaming and buttons announcing their disgust with drunk drivers. In a jury trial, these employees certainly should get tossed out of court, and it's not a bad idea to have your attorney sequester or otherwise remove them at *any* legal proceeding. It's tough enough for anyone to get justice in a drunk driving trial. The cop shouldn't be allowed to bring his cheerleaders into court.

Since we are talking about juries and what affects and impresses them, let's talk about your clothes, okay, big fella? There is a strong theory among defense lawyers that when a jury starts to dress the way your client does, you've got a winner. So if you get arrested for drunk driving and go to trial, when the jurors all show up wearing Nazi motorcycle helmets, you can pretty well figure that you have won them over. But I'll give you a last word of caution here about your Schwinn. In some states, drunk bicycling counts as drunk driving. If I were you, I'd take the baseball cards off your rear spokes. The cops might think you have a Honda.

My dad got arrested for drunk driving and the state took his license. If I buy him a moped to get around, will the pigs leave him alone?

Probably not. All states are strengthening their drunk driving laws to include other types of vehicles, particularly vehicles that don't require a driver's license like mopeds, golf carts, riding tractors and lawn mowers. You can drink beer and mow your grass so long as you stay on your own property, but drop one wheel off the curb and you can get busted for drunk driving. Many states are now charging for drunk riding while on horseback (see the Appendix).

It is a good idea to get your pop a designated driver instead. (Of course, we know who that will be.) But you have to look at the jeopardy if he gets arrested for driving *anything* while he has a driver's license suspension for a prior drunk driving offense. A conviction for driving, even if sober at the time of arrest, on a suspended license for drunk driving calls for automatic jail time in most states. If you want to keep your old man out of the cooler, it's better to buy him a new pair of tennis shoes.

I don't know why you say I shouldn't talk to the cop at a drunk driving stop. I sell used cars; I can talk my way out of anything.

Okay, let's go back and do this by the numbers. At every drunk driving arrest, the cop has to write a report. Usually half of it is pre-printed with boxes to check. The very first line usually is associated with the driver's demeanor. Was he ☐ talkative; ☐ responsive; ☐ combative; ☐ sullen; ☐ angry; ☐ silent?

Talkative is always correlated to excess drinking and *will* be introduced into evidence against you. No matter how well you handle booze or how good a communicator you are, it's best to shut up. Let the cop mark responsive or silent or whatever he wants, except talkative. Chatter is dangerous. Juries remember from their high school days how as kids they tried to talk their way out of trouble after a couple drinks... and it didn't work. They will look at you the same way. Hush!

Additionally, there are a few related issues that we should deal with regarding an initial stop by police. What if the cop is a woman? Here are two good guidelines: Treat her as a cop first and call her "officer." Don't hit on her, she's liable to hit back, and I mean unromantically. A professional nod will possibly keep you out of jail. "Hi toots!" and a wink will certainly bring you closer.

With all the problems cops carry onto the road, female cops carry even more baggage because it's assumed they can't do the job. The idea is that they are women, therefore, they are weak. It follows, then, that a good way to get your head cracked is to remind them of their sexuality. Just know that when you leave the barroom, you enter the cop's domain. Who do you think is going to win?

Now, there are other kinds of cops too, but the most dangerous is the kid cop. Where female cops don't give any breaks because *it's just not right*, kid cops whack everybody because they have an ax to grind with the world. Youth and ego might be a big part of it, but the real reason for their universal animosity is that they got jilted five years ago at the junior prom, so now everyone is going to pay. These guys are really dangerous. You must be careful with a kid cop because he's liable to execute you for running a stop sign. I mean it.

On the brighter side, older cops nearing retirement tend to be decent, even paternalistic in some circumstances, particularly with women offenders. Where middle-aged cops tend toward bounty hunting because they are always in a cash crunch, the older guys don't really need the money, have no cause to champion, have seen generations of drunk drivers come and go, and finally, they are just not completely satisfied that all the latest rule changes are for the best. They remember the days when they drove almost every drunk driver home instead of to the police station, when mailmen walked a route around their own neighborhoods and acted as a secondary beat man, when the only dope around was sitting in the chief's executive chair. Wasn't it great in 1928?

Finally, let's get racial. Black cops, and I think in a little lower percentage, Hispanics, are positively the best people to pull you over for drunk driving. They seem to instinctively understand that deals are part of the judicial system and that every drunk driver just doesn't need to get run the whole way out to the end of the line. If you get stopped by one of these guys, act decent and civil; you've got a chance. Just like with the older cops, you only hurt your chances by trying to whine a story on them. If your case is marginal, you have acted reasonably and been adult about it, these cops are probably leaning your way anyhow. Hush!

Until now you've talked only about getting pulled over on the road. What about drunk driving roadblocks? Are they legal and can I run them?

Yes and sometimes. Drunk driving roadblocks were ruled legal in 1990 (Michigan, Department of State Police v. Sitz, 489 U.S., 110 S. Ct. 2481 1990), but held subject to strict procedures. But it is not illegal to make a *non-abrupt* maneuver or turn away from the roadblock, although State cases are somewhat split on the issue. A driver who made a casual turn down a side street just ahead of the roadblock was ruled innocent of any violation. A driver who stopped behind a line of cars at a roadblock, then executed a series of turnaround maneuvers, then fled in the opposite direction was found guilty of avoiding the roadblock as well as drunk driving. The key phrase is *non-abrupt*, but the key idea is probably worth a try. At a drunk driving roadblock, you are going to get a close look and an up-close smell. If you have been drinking and you approach any roadblock, you should assume that it is set up for drunk driving purposes, and you should consider *safely* avoiding it. The real charge is drunk driving, and you are getting it if you stop. If you avoid the roadblock, it's possible the cops won't see you, won't chase you or won't shoot at you. (Just kidding. Cops are only allowed to shoot at fleeing felons. Drunk driving is a misdemeanor generally. Even kid cops sometimes won't shoot at you in this situation.)

Now that you have learned all this legal stuff, let's test your new knowledge and have a little quiz on the following "true" (no shit) traffic stop at a drunk driving roadblock.

A motorist waited in line at a night-time drunk driving roadblock. When it was his turn, he locked his car doors, but slipped a waiting officer his cards through a slight opening at the top of the window. The officer motioned him to wind down his window; the motorist refused, but turned on his interior lights. The officer then rapped on the window several times and yelled, "Get the ★?*! out of the car." The motorist shook his head sideways and pointed to his cards. The officer rapped and screamed again. A second officer approached from the passenger side and both officers shined bright flashlights at the motorist, whereupon he covered his head with his jacket. A third officer then shined a patrol car spotlight through the motorist's windshield. The first two officers then pocketed their flashlights and the motorist laid down on the floor of his vehicle. In a few minutes, an officer with a "slim jim" emergency car door opener began working on the driver's side door. After about five minutes, the door lock popped up, whereupon the motorist immediately re-locked it. The officers found after more tinkering that the lock had become damaged, and the door could not be re-opened from the outside with their device. They moved to the passenger side, and the motorist did the same. To their profane chagrin, the cops found that, once again, the door lock was damaged by their tinkering. By now, more police officers had to be dispatched to the scene to direct a half-mile long line of traffic that had backed up at the roadblock, and the roadblock purpose was by now abandoned.

There was a discussion among five officers where it was decided that the police would break the driver's side window with a nightstick, open the door and take custody of the uncooperative motorist. After several bashes on the window, the driver got behind the wheel, started the engine and, peeking through a slit in his jacket, began to nudge his car forward. An officer jumped in front of the car and yelled "Stop! Police!" The motorist stopped his vehicle. The cops started bashing at the window again, the motorist again nudged the car forward, this time bumping the cop in front. The officer then banged his nightstick on the car hood, swore, then smashed both car headlights. In the next moment, an officer with a shot-shell pistol blasted and flattened all four tires. It was pretty well agreed in testimony that, at this point, things were starting to get funny, but then the lieutenant arrived. He dispersed the troops but had the disabled vehicle hoisted onto a flatbed truck and taken into custody, with two police cars following. Somewhere en route, no one was sure where, the motorist unlocked a door and the nutty squirrel got away! He was arrested, with a warrant, a day later in his home and charged with:

1. Aggravated assault on police;
2. Drunk driving;
3. Avoiding a roadblock;
4. Endangering the safety of others;
5. Failure to obey a lawful order;
6. Inciting or promoting a riot;
7. Disorderly conduct;
8. Resisting arrest;
9. Reckless driving;
10. Fleeing police;
11. Failure to stop and identify;
12. Unlawful activities; and
13. Driving without lights to avoid police.

What do you think he was most likely convicted of?

Okay, let's reason the merits of this case like Supreme Court Justices. Who thinks the motorist is innocent on all counts? Raise your right hands. Yo! Rehnquist, your other right. Atta boy. Okay, let's count 'em: one, two, three, four, five votes for complete acquittal. That's a majority. The squirrel is innocent. Now who says the Supreme Court is packed with neo-nazi, pro-police, redneck conservatives?

The *real* decision in state court was similar. After listening to the testimony, defense and cross examination, the judge acquitted the motorist on all charges by the judge's own motion. Noting for the record that a medical doctor had testified that the defendant had an intense fear of police and a general phobia of all authority figures, the judge then picked apart each charge in the context of the motorist's actual conduct. Essentially, while the roadblock stop was lawful, practically everything the police did after the stop was not. The judge then opined that a police officer's duty is to "serve and protect," not break, enter and kidnap.

Police officers often lecture in elementary schools that the "policeman is your friend." Unless you are a young, attractive female, figure that this kind of attitude ends around the fifth grade, then watch out for the Rodney King autograph model electrical nightstick.

Whenever possible, it's best to avoid the police. I listened to a case once where a drunk driver was arrested after he stopped the cop and asked for directions. What is really scary is that this simpleton drives on the same roads as you and I. Even when he is not drunk, he's got to be dangerous.

Yeah, well, uh... I'm a better driver when I'm drinking or doing coke or smoking marihuana and... um... uh... I forgot what I was gonna say.

Okay, we can wait. We'll take another question.

Uh... no. It's okay; I got it now...

Well?

Uh... I forgot again.

Okay, we'll just...

No. I really got it this time... what... uh... what should I do like... uh... y'know, if I get stopped by the pigs, man?

Sneeze on them. They will back off, okay, dude? Go back on the nod, you can watch the tape later. I'll play it right after *The Munsters.*

Oh, wow, man, that's my favorite show!

I can dig it. Nite-nite. Anyone else have a question?

Is this guy for real?

Unfortunately, yes; and he thinks so too, but he has a lot of company. There is an army of horrific drivers out there who act and respond a lot like him. What is really unsettling is that most of them act that way normally and are under no influence except their own naturally bad selves. A maniac driver doesn't need to be on drugs or alcohol to be a highway menace. Most sixteen year olds, male and female, immediately qualify. They may have a baby-fresh driver's license, but their motoring skills are infantile as well. Add a quart of beer, and they give reasonable drunks like us a bad name. From what I hear in court, the tendency today is to get totally whacked at party time, and the party is always on. Forget the light beer, these kids want malt liquor bull, Mad Dog 20/20 and Yukon Jack. Then they do drugs. Then they cruise the strip or the Burger King obstacle course at 85 M.P.H. It is not a coincidence that most vehicular homicide cases I see involve drivers under 25 years old.

On the upper end of the menace scale are the retired drivers who don't know that they are retired yet. There is a quiet policy drifting among the states which requires automatic retesting of drivers as they age into the 65-70 year old category. These drivers generally have good intentions, but they are S-L-O-W. At some point in everyone's life, they come to realize that they just can't cut the mustard anymore, except when it comes to driving. People just seem to think they will be able to drive forever. It ain't so. Every year, I see about a dozen ninety-plus year old men hobble into court to plead against a license revocation. Their claim is always the same: Take away their license and they will die. They do anyway, some within weeks of their hearing. Death may be the one true fact of life, but it's better that they die in bed, not at a school bus stop after they drove down the sidewalk and scattered all the little bowling pins.

From the young to the old, we go now to the plain stupid. I have maintained for years that the first prerequisite for a driver's test should be an I.Q. test. Still, for no logical reason, our roads are cluttered with wrecks caused by otherwise intelligent people. They pull into oncoming traffic, blow through red lights, and bump their way onto the freeway at seventy miles an hour. They believe that their brakes will always work at the last second, and they read the road signs after they pass them. Yield? What the hell does *that* mean? Honest to God, I have listened to cases where men reading the newspaper while driving didn't believe they were guilty of careless driving.

Traffic laws today don't mean very much. Speed limits, red lights, stop signs and related violations have all become breakable laws and all bring fierce defenses: "The light was yellow, I don't speed, I stopped for the sign, the cop must be mistaken."

Add a touch of alcohol to otherwise bad driving habits and the results are predictable. There will be arrests, first for barrelling through the stop sign, then for drunk driving and finally for killing someone in the crossing lane. It very well may be that some people are better drivers after they have been drinking. They are more careful when under the influence because they recognize the danger they face if arrested. If they are going to get home, they have got to be sneaky, and sneaky means planned, careful driving. At least, that is what a reasonable drunk driver should think.

Alcohol blurs vision, numbs the senses, slows reaction time, disrupts brain activity, clumps the red blood cells into a flat sticking goo causing drowsiness and encourages irresponsibility. It's natural then that some people think they can drive better after drinking.

If I get arrested and I get a specialized drunk driving lawyer, will I have to mortgage my house to pay him?

Only if you killed somebody, and you were charged with vehicular homicide or manslaughter on top of the drunk driving charge. I'll give you some ballpark figures. A charge of vehicular homicide always carries the threat of years in prison, so intense fear is a natural reaction to the bad news. When a lawyer smells fear, he will charge accordingly. As he tries to compute the highest price he thinks you will readily pay, he is sizing up your emotions against the sales price. If you are scared shitless, he will ask for $25,000, even though $10,000 is a fairer price for this kind of trial, not including a couple grand for accident reconstruction expert witnesses. For a normal drunk driving trial only, three to five thousand dollars is about right.

But most drunk driving charges in America are lodged against first offenders. Because the courts and jails are swamped with criminals anyway, state legislatures have devised alternative sentencing procedures for first offender drunk drivers. This gets them placed out of the criminal system quickly; they serve no jail time and their names are off the books in six months to a year. Alternative sentencing procedures require no special effort on the lawyer's part. He is there to hold your hand and walk you through the process. Sometimes it gets to be an assembly line. I often see the same lawyer on sentencing day dragging four, five, a half dozen different defendants before the court. One after another, they plead and get the same sentence: a $500 fine and costs, six months probation, two months loss of license. It's like saying the rosary: nothing changes.

But it's profitable for the lawyer. The fee for a simple, pre-arranged plea or alternative sentencing hearing should be around $250. Unless the lawyer has done or promised more than appearing at this one event, if his fee is higher, he's a dog robber. And in this circumstance, yes, your cousin Vinnie's divorce lawyer or your idiot brother-in-law, the lawyer, will be suitable counsel. All the lawyer is doing in this circumstance is accepting the district attorney's offer, a plea bargain so to speak, and walking you to the bench. You can do that yourself and, in many states, it's encouraged, or at least not discouraged, that you appear without counsel. BUT! Just after you are arrested you should get the initial advice of an experienced drunk driving lawyer because you might be able to beat the system altogether. Pay the one hundred dollar consultation fee and ask him: "What are my chances?" He can't fib, but he can't guess either, it's unethical. But at some point after he goes through all the bullshit about "you never know what a judge or jury is going to do," you'll be able to gauge your own chances.

Finally, if you sign on with a lawyer, ask him to charge an hourly fee and give you an inventory and billing notices. A hundred dollars an hour is generous, ninety is more like it. Since everything is done in court, and the system in place is self-generating (see the judge, go to the probation office, sign up for counseling, okay, we'll call you in two weeks), the lawyer has no documents to prepare and no real work to perform. He is there to nod when the judge asks if you know your rights and not much more. If the lawyer can find a way to bill you for over two hours at a sentencing hearing, you are paying for his men's room stop on the way *out* of the courthouse. When dealing with lawyers, always keep both eyes on your poochie.

I can't get a record out of this, can I? It will kill my job.

You can, but it doesn't have to last. There is a legal procedure called expungement; it's fairly simple, not costly, and highly recommended for everyone *ever* charged with drunk driving. If you were convicted of a D.U.I. charge ten years ago, you can still have your record expunged. Unfortunately, it takes a lawyer to file your paperwork, but it doesn't require a hearing usually, so the process is cheap. Court costs plus legal fees are still under two hundred bucks.

An expungement is a court order to destroy the records of your case and conviction after you have successfully been released from probation. There will be a residual notice of conviction left with your traffic safety department and other law enforcement types, but only for the purpose of enhanced grading if you get whacked again. If you gave fingerprints, and they went on the F.B.I. computer, likewise, they will remain as will a record of your conviction. The F.B.I. expunges nothing and has no respect for a state court order. But they can only share the notice of your record with other cops or use it for their own purposes of domestic spying. Newspapers, employers, private investigators, even corporate nazis are prohibited from gaining access to an expunged record. By order of court, it doesn't exist, so they can't even discuss it.

I want to know about the new laws on commercial driving. I boss the big rig, and I don't mean my old lady. I'm mighty pissed at how they are always picking on us truckers.

Well, good buddy. . .Hey! Sit down, man, I was just kidding. Okay, Okay, I'll tell you about it.

Commercial drivers are riding on the wave of the future, and the wave is breaking bad for everybody. If there was any fear that pressure is still out there to further reduce blood alcohol levels for drunk driving, the new commercial driving laws are proof.

The federal *Commercial Motor Vehicle Safety Act of 1986* is now in the process of being adopted by all states. Not only does it standardize enforcement procedures state to state for all commercial drivers no matter where they are registered or licensed, it generally reduces the blood alcohol concentration to .04 for conviction of drunk driving. Figure that as about one-half of what it takes to convict an automobile driver. A conviction means you lose your commercial license and your job for one year. Now here is the shocker. Some states are applying this standard against you even if you are off duty and in your private vehicle. If you have a commercial driver's license, it doesn't matter *what* you are driving, the penalties are being recorded against your license, not your vehicle.

Further, if there is a detection of any alcohol in your system while on duty, you will be put off the road for 24 hours. So, if you drink an O'Douls non-alcoholic beverage, you can get shut down immediately because the cop smells *beer*. This situation is going to cause a whole new twist to the old farmer's daughter jokes. At least our nation's traveling salesmen should be thankful.

Anyone who drives a motor vehicle weighing over 26,000 pounds, including school buses, comes under the proposed jurisdiction of commercial drivers licensing. The idea behind the law is to get the gypsies off the road, professionalize the entire trucker corps and make heavy hauling a career, not a hobby. It therefore follows that no one escapes enforcement for any traffic offense, no matter in what state the violation is committed. My advice is, if you don't absolutely, positively, really, really need a commercial license, you are better off without it. In this case, leave the driving and the increased scrutiny to somebody else, except maybe Greyhound bus drivers until the real ones come off strike.

I heard that drunk driving laws are getting so tough that you can get arrested even if you are not driving. Is that so?

It's true, and I have already told you about the first way: When you pull off the road or climb into your car in the parking lot, leave the keys in the ignition and fall asleep. Even though the car isn't running, the law recognizes that you are in "actual, physical control" of the vehicle, so you can get pulled out of the vehicle and arrested without driving.

The second way comes under the traffic statutes that make it illegal for you to "permit a violation," and every state has this kind of law. Let's say that you have been drinking for several hours, and you know that you are totally kicked in the ass. Your car has been in the tavern parking lot since early afternoon, and you remember that your wife needs it by seven o'clock. If you could walk and if you could find your car... nah, maybe you still shouldn't drive. But you must get your car home soon, so you ask the next available drunk for a favor. "Hey, Louie, I'll give you ten bucks to drive my car home. My wife'll drop you back here on her way to bingo."

You pass out in the passenger seat and Louie drives your car. But as he bends over to light his cigarette, the car veers across the highway and chases an oncoming motorcyclist into a tree, sandwiching bike and rider between your car and the sturdy oak. The biker, of course, is more than cold-cocked. He has been thoroughly cooled. The police can't waken you, so they send you off to the hospital where you wake the next morning, unhurt and unknowledgeable of the wreck. Louie's blood alcohol content registered at .12 percent. He was arrested for drunk driving and vehicular homicide. During his interview, Louie said that he had been drinking with you for a couple hours and that you paid him to drive your car home. Additionally, it didn't take the rat long to start growing a tail, because Louie mentioned that you knew he was drunk as well, but probably not as drunk as you. Two days later, the police arrest you under the permitting statutes for drunk driving and vehicular homicide.

Even though you weren't driving, you could be guilty of the same charges as the driver if the prosecutor can show knowledge on your part that Louie was drunk and that you consented to his driving in an illegal manner. In this case, if knowledge of Louie's drunkenness is proved against you, consent steps right alongside. Even though you slept through the whole thing, if Louie gets convicted, you are going to share his jail cell.

If you need a driver, when you look around the barroom, choose wisely, but choose someone who is in the Pepsi generation. And make sure he has a driver's license. You could pay fines on this as well.

I have a little decal on my window that says "Fraternal Order of Police." It cost me fifteen bucks as a donation. Now the cops aren't supposed to arrest me, right?

Your sticker is worthless. Cops usually ignore them, as well as the courtesy card that goes with it. Wake up, this is the nineties. You can't buy your way out of anything for fifteen bucks.

The story behind F.O.P. courtesy stickers has become tainted. As a fund-raising tool for the police union, the sale of decals was effective in years past but has recently been exposed as misleading, if not dishonest. The telephone soliciting company keeps about 75 percent of the money they raise harassing you on the cops' behalf. The police union knows it is being ripped off. The cops know they are being ripped off and the media has exposed the fund-raising as a rip-off. If everyone knows that the decal is a joke, the joke then is on you if you try to exploit it. Besides, drunk driving is too serious an offense to ask for a little courtesy. What I have been seeing over the past few years with increasing frequency is cops arresting cops. Hell, I know of a bounty hunter who waited down the road from the annual police picnic. He got three suspects before some drunks stole his cop car and ran it into the lake.

If the cops don't respect a cop sticker, they likewise ignore clergy, medical-related and military emblems. Read the papers (but don't necessarily believe them). Everyone and anyone can be arrested for drunk driving. But you never drink? You would be amazed at what products contain alcohol. Cough syrup or breath spray plus a little erratic driving is enough to get you pulled over and tested for booze.

But... if you have a badge, whip it out. I have never badged my way out of a drunk driving charge, but it has worked on numerous speeding violations. A badge still commands respect, but you can't let the cop know you have been drinking. Stay in your car as the officer approaches, hands high on the wheel, badge opened on the dashboard. When he comes alongside the window, badge him immediately, but don't engage in much conversation.

You don't have a badge? Have one made. There are bunches of vacant chicken scratch, but authoritarian, positions available for the asking at the state, county and municipal levels. Some of them carry real law enforcement power: Animal Control Officer, Deputy Constable, Volunteer Fire Policemen, Assistant Game Warden, Deputy Fish Commissioner, Auxiliary Deputy Sheriff, Deputy Fire Marshall, Deputy Coroner, Deputy Dawg. The funny thing is, real police, even state police, have to use these people sometime. What is a real cop to do if he has to investigate a dead body covered with rattlesnakes, found in a fire trap, protected by a rabid rottweiler? Easy, he first calls the Assistant Auxiliary Deputy Animal Control Officer Coroner Fire Marshal Game Warden Policeman. They do the dirty work while the real cop summons the newspaper photographers.

The idea is, any badge is worthwhile. If the cop has not immediately decided to arrest you, he may pause to remember that, "Oh yeah, this is the guy I call to pick up dead deer on the highway."

A badge gives you an edge because there is a real policeman-like job attached to it. Cops can respect this because the sub-cop jobs are usually shit details, and because those sub-cop jobs exist, real cops don't have to do them. Volunteer firemen, not Republicans, run the country. It's just that, for right now, the Republicans have their number. Get a badge, but not one that says "Press." Remember, judges hate reporters, and cops don't like anybody very much.

What about, like, if I got my kids in the car with me? Will that keep me from gettin' busted?

I hope not, but, unfortunately, it may. Cops *do* like little kids. They act like them enough. But it may also get you a felony charge of endangering the welfare of snots if the cop nails you for careening down the sidewalk shit-faced with a car full of ragamuffins hanging out the windows. Let's face it. Some cops are heartless pricks.

The reason you might get away with drunk driving in this instance is that, if the cop takes you in, he must also arrest your kids. Now he has a bunch of bad-ass kindergarten thugs running about the police station until he can get mama or a relative, if there is one, or get the kids placed in a shelter, which takes a couple light years. Kids hanging around the police station keep the cops honest. A cop's jerk-off time gets reduced to zero. He has to keep his uniform and weapon on his person and watch that the kids don't sneak into the evidence/narcotics room and steal the department's private stash. Kids are a big pain in the ass and cops know it. Unless you are really smashed, there is a fair chance that a cop won't take you and the kidlets off to the pokey.

But there is one other significant reason why you should not drink and drive with your kids along. Even if you make it safely home and act out your best imitation of a god-fearin', teetotallin', cross-bearin', righteous Christian, one of the little dorks will likely pop off, "Mom, Dad drank twenty-seven beers. I counted every one of them."

You know, you judges aren't perfect either. I think a lot of guys bite the dust just because the judge had a bad day around the office, okay?

Right. And all the guys in jail are innocent, just ask them.

The fact is, nobody is perfect. That is why a drunk driver generally is entitled to a trial by jury... that way he can be put in jail by committee.

There are crusader rabbits in all walks of life. If arrested, you just have to hope one doesn't hop in front of you in the court-room. Your lawyer will know if you get a MADD judge, and he should petition the court for a recusal or change of venue. If the judge refuses your lawyer's request, your lawyer can appeal. Don't get excited about the cost yet. These are procedural matters routinely dealt with in the courthouse. Often, an appeal of this nature is included in the original fee that you have paid.

But understand that there are MADD judges waiting out there to hit you unusually hard. I know of one who brags about it on the lecture circuit. In his courtroom, drunk drivers face maximum penalties, even on plea bargains and pre-arranged deals. Naturally, even the district attorney's office despises him because he is upsetting the system. As a fellow jurist, I guess I can understand a crusade here and there, and I probably wouldn't be offended by this guy, except that I know the hypocrite drinks and drives.

The problem I see with these crucifix-carrying reformers is that they don't apply their own faith to themselves. A holier than thou attitude is okay if you really are holier than thou. I ain't seen one yet. The only *Saints* I have ever seen play professional football out of New Orleans.

Just as you have to run MADD cheerleaders out of the courtroom, you can't let a MADD judge face you down either. There is an old Russian proverb, "It's not the law you must fear, but the judge." Bank on that one. The law, even if unequally applied, is still neutral. The battle is between the prosecutor and your lawyer. Now in theory the prosecutor's job is only to see that the truth comes out, and the trial issues are fairly presented. In practice though, the prosecutor wants to pad his won-lost record, and he'll throw a curve ball on every pitch in order to win. Don't count on the district attorney being your friend; he is there to hang you.

Now, if the prosecutor is determined to pitch a win against you at all costs, you can't let a MADD judge be the umpire. It is difficult enough for a drunk driver just walking into any courtroom. You are a defendant. Don't believe the crap about being innocent until proved guilty. Drunk driving laws presume you guilty until proved innocent. An accused drunk driver already stands before the jury in a bad light because he has been arrested. He must have done *something* wrong, okay? I can tell you that half the people in any jury pool have a pre-conceived notion that the criminal defendant is guilty, and now he is trying to weasel out of his crime. It is up to the judge to make them forget that notion. It is the judge's job to oversee a fair trial. If your judge is an anti-drunk driving crusader, a public lecturer or a crack-down artist and you allow him to manage *your* day in court, you leave yourself only two options: Plead guilty or take the bridge. Either way, the judge is going to make you jump. Get away from him.

With all the advances in medicine and technology, don't they have a pill that can sober you up real fast so that you can drive?

Just as there are only two cures for seasickness, land and death, there are only two ways to sober up rapidly: (1) Get ten hours sleep; or (2) Die. Massive doses of Vitamin B complex might get you through a hangover, but only sleep and time can cure drunkenness.

Alcohol shoots through the body within a half hour after drinking and gets a head start into the bloodstream as it leaches through the stomach walls. About ten to twelve percent of the alcohol consumed soon leaves the body through the urine, sweat and breath evaporation. The rest circulates through the system and is gradually broken down as it passes through the liver. If the liver is healthy, it is capable of processing and detoxifying about one drink an hour. It ain't enough. Many people wake up, not only with a hangover, but with considerable amounts of alcohol still in the system. They slept six hours, and they are still drunk.

Alcohol is poisonous and can kill. A .4 drunk should be in a coma and a .5 should be dead. Still, I've seen articulate people come in for arraignment on their own after registering .5 plus. The prototype seems to be tall, skinny, white girls who do both alcohol and cocaine which keeps their systems jolted awake, but I've also seen a husky coal miner who, at .61 and climbing, could reasonably understand questions and articulate answers.

There is also some validity to the idea that a person can drink himself sober. Since alcohol is water-soluble, it is unevenly absorbed by different parts of the body as it mixes in the arterial bloodstream. Soft organs, such as the brain, will absorb alcohol faster than muscle tissue. Until a maximum concentration of alcohol has been uniformly distributed through the body, a drinker may appear slush-mouthed and woozy on just a few drinks, then appear reasonably sober a half hour later as the alcohol in his system reaches equilibrium in all parts of the body. He appears to have sobered up while he was drinking. Since the ingestion of food slows down the absorption of alcohol, an apparent drunk can appear recovered in a short time by eating a meal even while he drinks.

On the other side, water accelerates the effects of alcohol and so gives strength to the anti-hangover water trick. For years, it has been a proven tactic of steelworkers I know: gobble four aspirin, then guzzle four glasses of water when the bars close. They will wake with a diminished hangover and report on time for the 8:00 a.m. to 4:00 p.m. mill shift. Of course, they are back asleep at 9:00 a.m., but not because of a hangover. I think it's on-the-job stress or something.

The point here is that if alcohol can be pushed out of the body a little early by drinking water, why not switch to water only, an hour or so before you leave the bar? It might dilute the alcohol concentration enough to bring a later chemical test reading below your state's magic number that indicates "drunk driver."

What! And miss last call? No way, Man. Water is what you piss in. I'll have another Double-Jack with a Heine on the side... and I will be at the speakeasy at 4:00 a.m. Later, Dude.

Okay. If water is not in your diet, you should still consider taking a massive dose of aspirin, but take the aspirin at the very end of the party. There is some evidence that aspirin, and similarly, acetaminophen (Tylenol, Advil, etc.) will *enhance* intoxication when taken during a bout of drinking alcohol. But there is other evidence that says aspirin taken at the end of drinking tends to reduce your body temperature and therefore can lower your apparent blood alcohol reading on a breath test by 10 percent to 20 percent. Of course, you might get the same effect by drinking your last two for the road while sitting on the floor of the beer cooler, but remember, breath tests are not measured using rectal air. As well, refrigeration makes it difficult to ignite.

If there is no medical pill that can quickly sober me up, what about a home remedy?

The cure is in prevention. Alcohol seeps from the stomach into the small intestine then into the bloodstream where the heart pumps it finally into the brain. Whamo! This is where the problems of intoxication begin. If you could keep the booze out of your noggin, you could drink forever and not get a drunken effect... But aside from taking the guillotine about twenty minutes after you started drinking, there is no way to shortstop the biological process. The idea then is to slow down the advancing army.

Greeks use olive oil to coat their stomachs before drinking, Italians like melted butter with garlic (it throws off the scent), the Irish chew up half a potato field before they start and yuppies like Vitamin B-12 and bee pollen. While it has been shown that Vitamin B-12 will help wash the bloodstream as a hangover cure, the merits of bee pollen are still debated, and one major demerit is evident: bee pollen can test positive for amphetamines in the blood sample. Still, there might be something to it. People have thought the world was flat much longer than they knew it was round. But there is a word of caution on taking bee pollen, read the package carefully and don't confuse it with wasp pollen. While bee pollen *may* have some anti-intoxication advantages, wasp pollen will only create an urge to attend a

Presbyterian Church. Next question. How about the little old man with the wild hand in the middle row.

I would like to get an artificial penis. I am not able to get an erection anymore, and I think my wife would enjoy a little action. She is only 83 years old. Do you know of a company that sells fakes?

Uh... I hate to tell you, Pops, but the seminar on sex and aging is two doors down the hall. If you limp on over there, they might get you straightened out.

My neighbor is a drunk driver. He's wrecked into my fence, driven through my garden and run over my dog... and he called me a pussy. What can I do about him?

Call 911. While cops are usually never around when you need them, they are obliged to respond to a call that reports a suspected drunk driver. As well, the MADD women, and some insurance companies and civic groups, have set up drunk driver hotlines to keep the cops continually hustling after fleeing shadows.

But it is not altogether proper to make an arrest yourself. If you screw up and the guy is sober, you can be charged with criminal restraint and sued right down to your foreskin. The cry of "citizen's arrest!" went out with Gomer Pyle chasing Barney Fife off the television. Volunteerism is risky.

Still, it is permissible to hold a drunk at an accident scene and quasi-police (firemen, constables, game wardens) have arrest powers in many circumstances regarding a drunk driver. While any driver, drunk or sober, is entitled to the constitutional protections of privacy and probable cause *while driving*, these protections are greatly diminished after a wreck or when the drunk has exited his vehicle. This doesn't give you the right to cause the wreck or to run him off the road or to unceremoniously yank him out of his car, but I think any jury would be sympathetic to the citizen who disarmed a drunk driver by taking his keys or who kept him from fleeing a serious traffic accident. However, know that there are limits and everybody these days has their rights.

What if I get pulled over, and I have a gun in my car?

Yikes! You must be from California, dude: you're talking about standard equipment.

Traffic cops have a love-hate relationship with guns; they love theirs, they hate yours. Remember that every cop at every traffic stop is first thinking "gun" before anything else. If he finds one, you are in for a serious hassle even if the gun is legal, and you have a permit. Keep it hidden.

A cop is permitted to frisk you for his own safety at any traffic stop. Hiding the gun on your person is not a good place. A cop is permitted to make a "sight search" of articles in "plain view" in your vehicle when he stops you, to look for guns, contraband and drugs. But cops, like cats, are curious critters. They are always trying to go into forbidden places. Glove compartments, trunks and closed containers are always worth an illegal look. If the cop finds something, fine, you are under arrest, and he can untangle the mess later in the courthouse. You should win, but in the meantime, he has your gun.

If the cop finds nothing, so what? It's his word versus yours on what got searched, and if the cop is backed against the wall, he will always say that you consented to the search. If the cop *asks* for your consent, then you know that he is not legally permitted to look without a search warrant. But the truth is, no place is a safe place to keep a gun in your car.

If your gun is hidden *out of sight*, the best advice is to take your chance. Let the cop play his games, but don't consent to a search. No matter how much he threatens or accuses, he is bluffing. He doesn't have enough information to get a search warrant and your refusal alone is nothing more than suspicious. If he finds your gun, your lawyer can have the evidence (the gun itself) suppressed and the gun charge dismissed.

If you are wearing a gun, even legally, the circumstances get dangerous. People have been shot for less. You cannot let the cop discover the gun for himself, that risks a pistol-whipping. If it looks like you are going to be frisked, look directly into the cop's eyes, *slowly* raise both hands over your head and say: "Officer, under my left arm, I am wearing a gun." Try to add: "The permit is in my wallet," before the cop freaks out. But if the traffic stop is routine, shut-up and wait the cop out. Don't confess anything unless he is getting ready to grope you.

What if the cop does get a search warrant? I mean, I might have more than just a gun in the car.

In that case, you are in for a long haul. The cop is going to get whatever is in the vehicle, wherever it is hidden.

Search warrants permit the ultimate invasion of your privacy. Forget your home and car, a cop armed with a search warrant can go into your body. He can take your blood, probe your cavities (I don't mean teeth), ram exotic instruments up your gigi. (Make sure he doesn't have his hands on the back of your shoulders on this one, it may be his *own* instrument.) A cop with a search warrant can look for your *soul*, but he must convince a judge that he has probable cause for the search before he goes hunting.

There is good and bad news here. The law on probable cause is so strict that it means the cop's request almost certainly has to result in a successful search: Bye-bye gun, bye-bye dope, bye-bye hidden Mexican aliens on dope armed with guns. A good probable cause nearly always results in a good search. But bad search warrants are issued every day. This is because the process of issuance is generally entrusted to the lowest rung of the judiciary: squires, justices of the peace, magistrates, people with a rank just above notary public.

The problem here is not so much that they are unsuitably trained (that may be a sub-problem). The danger is that they are too damned cozy with the cops. Anyone who has ever gone into a local court for a speeding ticket has seen the problem: cops behind the secretary's counter, feet up, slurping coffee; cops with the judge, ogling pictures of the latest deer kill; cops hanging over the secretary's shoulders, analyzing the woman's... uh ...typing skills. In this kind of courthouse, you wait for the judge's call: "Send the next guilty person into my courtroom."

Here, when a judge can choose so easily between two human beings, it is somewhat pre-decided that a local judge will sign off on a cop's bad search warrant, especially when the victim is not there to contest it.

I have reviewed search warrants issued with the following probable cause:

1. "Somebody said he's got dope growing in his bedroom."

2. "A green car like his was spotted near the Agway when it was robbed, so it's a pretty good chance he did it."

3. "The guy wouldn't take out his contact lenses when I asked if he was wearing them since his license said he needed glasses. I want a search warrant to yank them out myself."

How would you like to be on the wrong end of search warrant number 3? If the driver was a suspected drunk as well, the cop could give his eye sockets a blood test, just so long as he requested the test on the search warrant. You see, even in a court where substantive and constitutional laws are ignored, you still have to follow procedure.

If someone "stone sober" runs into a joint, downs six rapid shots and a couple quick beers and is gone in ten minutes, if immediately pulled over, is he drunk?

Even though alcohol's effects may kick in within fifteen minutes or so, it takes about one-half hour for the alcohol to sufficiently circulate into the body to indicate any substantial percentage, and equilibrium throughout the body may not occur for a couple hours. Therefore, the body's blood alcohol concentration hasn't maximized until long after the drinking has stopped. That is why most drunk drivers show a *rising* percentage at the time of testing. Since testing is never contemporaneous with drinking, it happens every day that a driver is legally sober when he leaves the bar, is legally sober when he is stopped fifteen minutes down the road, is legally sober when he is taken to the hospital or police station and is legally drunk when he finally takes the test. Look at the sap in our introductory scenario. One and a half hours after he left the bar, he was barely but legally drunk, according to his state's statute. I admit that this might be an extreme example, but it makes a valid statement. Sometimes you just can't know "when to say when."

In the case of our man above who pounds eight drinks in ten minutes (I have seen this done, without spillage), he is not drunk when he gets into his car, but he'd better live nearby because he is going to be drunk, soon. If he gets stopped, he has only one option... stall the test. The alcohol in his blood is rising and will continue to rise for at least an hour. After it peaks, the alcohol will burn off at a speculative, approximate but not uniform rate of .015 percent an hour and may be higher depending on the individual's metabolism and particular absorption rate. Depending on a whole bunch of factors, it's possible that a couple hour delay in testing can bring his alcohol content below the state's magic line.

But how do you otall a breath test when the cop has his night stick halfway up your wazoo? There are several ways. As your lawyer, I advise you, when taken to the station, to get sick as soon as the cops rig up the breath machine. I mean it: barf, throw up, toss your waffle. There is a valid reason for this. The alcohol in your belly is still percolating into your blood system. If you burp, belch, fart or throw up just prior to blowing into the tube, the likelihood is that you are giving stomach or digestive air rather than a lung sample. Since stomach air does not reflect your true blood alcohol content and usually shows a much higher percentage of alcohol in your system, if you throw up, the law says you get time to settle down ...about twenty minutes. Now the law also says that the cops have to watch you for about twenty minutes anyway *before* they give you a breath test because they don't want you eating, drinking, smoking or throwing up during the pre-test period. These actions can contaminate the breath sample. So wait until just before you go on the box before you become ill. That tacks more time on since the cops have to restart the whole process after you vomit.

You can probably get away with this tactic a couple times before the cop despairs and writes you up as an *implied consent refusal* that suspends your driver's license. Cops give a lot of leeway to sick drunks because first, they may have to clean up the mess; and second, the room where breath tests are given is the cop's playpen. It is where they eat, smoke, drink, play cards and entertain friends while they serve and protect. No cop with any sense of class wants to spark with his girlfriend amid the odor of a reconstituted chicken wing and curly fries casserole with a side of cheese puffs and hard-boiled eggs, all half-baked in a seasoned *Old Milwaukee* sauce.

Here is a general rule: if you are marched in for a breath test, delay but don't obstruct. If the cop gets wind that you are not really ill because the charade is too obvious, he is going to mark you as a refusal. At some point, you must take the test or risk losing your driver's license for about a year. Take it only when you are forced or threatened... and save the plastic mouth piece, even if you have to steal it. Your lawyer can have it analyzed for foreign matter (waffle shrapnel) that will show the breath sample was contaminated with stomach particles and was not a true indication of the deep air in your lungs.

Additionally, there is another valid reason to stall the chemical test. Let's say you took your last drink at 11:15 p.m., got stopped by the cops at 11:30 p.m. and got tested at 12:45 a.m. The police need to show that your test score at 12:45 a.m. corresponds to your presumed drunken condition an hour and a half prior. They do this by having an "expert" testify that according to his charts and graphs, the "average" man would have a prior "estimated" blood alcohol reading in the illegal zone.

For a lot of reasons, this "retrograde extrapolation theory" is bullshit and your lawyer will prove it. Essentially, one chemical sample, blood, breath or urine, cannot tell the "expert" enough to know what your prior level was. He can't know if your alcohol level was rising or falling when tested, whether all the alcohol in your system had been fully absorbed and how much alcohol had already been eliminated from the bloodstream. Alcohol testing is usually limited to one test, or two, taken minutes apart, so it is you versus the single reading. One blood alcohol pinpoint on the expert's map can't possibly show a drunk or sober direction.

That means that the longer you stretch the time of testing away from the time of arrest, the more the "expert" has to stretch his one pinpoint across the whole map. He just can't do it. Even with two back to back tests, the results are going to be so similar, say a .12 and .13, that they are meaningless for the purpose of back-figuring a prior blood alcohol content. If they aren't similar, something is wrong with the machine. Any result on the same test sequence that shows more than a .02 difference in the two blows must, by law, be disregarded and the machine taken out of service. But the police then have a right to give you an additional blood or urine test. Some days you just can't win.

My boyfriend won't allow me to eat when we go drinking because he doesn't want me to pork up. I'm always on a diet anyway so what should I do when I go partying?

Eat. Lay off the booze. Dump your boyfriend, I can see that you will have future problems with this dickhead. You oughta dump him while you can.

Let me say it one last time: if you are going to drink, you have to eat. Preferably eat something substantial about one-half hour before drinking, to slow alcohol absorption. You must put something between you and the enemy. Meat and potatoes works best. Any protein or carbohydrate foods will slow down the effects of alcohol, while foods high in fat, like deep fried nerf nuggets, will just give the booze a dumb look and let it pass. While milk is excellent as a stomach coating, its fat content and bulk soon break down against the press of alcoholic acids and its effects are temporary. Real food is best. Eat pasta, bread, potatoes and meats before drinking. Lay off the chicken wings and junk foods. Eat a cheeseburger. Forget the diet. Remember this: you can lose weight later, on your own schedule. Everyone I ever saw who came out of a term in jail was a lot thinner than when they went in. If you don't eat and you drink enough to score above your state's magic number for "screwed up," it's going to cost you a lot more than a few pounds.

There are other considerations. You might catch "grog blossoms." I knew a man who shunned food because it "interfered with the buzz." He would eat one-half cheeseburger a day in between drinking 20-plus bottles of beer. As a custom, he got drunk three times a day. At 38 years old, his face, arms and chest exploded with acne-like sores that would not heal. He was dead of a blood disorder at age 40. It was a common death among beer and ale drunks of the Revolutionary War era, men who subsisted almost solely on brew; hence the name "grog blossoms" for the affliction of alcoholics who never ate.

Here is another question on me. Can you be arrested for drunk driving when you haven't been drinking?

The answer is yes. There are approximately 200 compounds that can be detected on the human breath. Some give off the same signals as alcohol (ethanol) to most breath analysis machines and therefore result in an artificial blood alcohol reading. While the machines are generally designed to be "specific for alcohol," they often identify any chemical associated with or belonging to the methyl group. The machine *assumes* that the other compounds are molecules of ethyl alcohol (ethanol). Acetone is one such compound and it is present in the breath of non-intoxicated subjects: diabetics, people on low protein or low carbohydrate diets and some victims of lung cancer. Recent research on non-drinking lung cancer patients' breath indicates that the organic chemicals, acetone, methylethyl-ketone and n-propanol will show on a breath sample using mass spectrometers and gas chromatographs, the same equipment that the cops use to gauge your blood alcohol content... *AND*...all three of the above chemicals will test positive for alcohol consumption.

It gets worse. Another chemical that gives positive readings for alcohol in the breath and blood is acetaldehyde, an alcohol byproduct that has routinely been detected in the breath of tobacco smokers, hard drunks (even when not drinking), pregnant women and women on steroid contraceptives. Translation: these people are more likely to have inflated blood alcohol readings whether they were drinking or not.

People who *have* been drinking, although not really intoxicated, may go over the legal limit because of the prior reasons or simply because they are ill and running a fever. A body temperature of 102 degrees can increase a moderate drinker's blood-alcohol reading by as much as 25 percent due to the increased volatility of the alcohol. In this instance, several heavy slugs of cough medicine could put you in harm's way before you get back from the drug store.

Blood testing is not perfect either. The truth is that many blood samples are taken after sterilizing the skin with an alcohol solution and thus contaminating the sample prior to removing it. Even so, a clean sample can create its own alcohol when it ferments in the test tube. Because of enzymes at work in the decaying action, alcohol is created in the blood. Research has shown that original, non-alcoholic samples can produce a "rotted" reading two to three times the .10 standard. Refrigeration slows the decomposition and some preservatives will halt it, but laboratories are pretty busy places, so often the blood sample doesn't get analyzed until several days after its withdrawal.

Urine samples can create alcohol even *after* preservatives have been added. A common yeast that forms in the urine causes the sample to break down and create alcohol, *AND* the yeast is immune to sodium fluoride, the most commonly used preservative. In the bladder, the same yeast *Candida Albicans*, when mixed with glucose, can create enough alcohol by itself to result in drunkenness. This is independent of *any* alcohol consumption by the test subject. Ain't that a pisser?

Finally, in any situation where you were either not drinking or barely drinking or you *know* that you weren't drunk and you still get hauled in by the cops for a chemical test, it is in your best interests to immediately thereafter and as soon as possible *get your own blood tested*. The cops will not give you a second test. Period. But you can go by yourself to a doctor, a hospital, a laboratory or a vampire and have your own sample taken and tested. If your blood test is even higher than the cop's blood test, you don't have to tell them. If your blood test is lower, then your lawyer can use the new information to your benefit.

You say get another blood test if I know I'm not drunk. How the hell am I going to know that? I wouldn't drive if I knew I was drunk.

Sure. And I'll bet you don't speed either... your speedometer was broken, you had it on cruise control at 55, your car doesn't go fast enough to speed. I've heard *all* the excuses.

The truth is, under the *per se* laws that *presume* you guilty if you register above the legal limit, you have to assume that any drinking is close enough to danger. It doesn't take all that much alcohol to hit a .10. Still... if you have been drinking for awhile and you don't make *obvious* social mistakes, such as sitting down where there is no chair, attempting to lean against objects that give under a little pressure (light bulbs, dutch doors, William Kennedy Smith) or emerging from the rest room with your tallywhacker clenched in your zipper, then you might still be sober enough to legally drive.

But, if you start up a conversation, meaning to say "Good evening, ladies, may I buy you a drink," but it comes out "Grazzer blat shish ma rinker, coupla sluts," anyone except you could reasonably *know* that you are drunk. *Or* if a friend tells you "Man, that redhead at the corner table really has the hots for you" and you believe him, you should give yourself a sobriety test as soon as you clean the redhead's drink off your face. *Or* if Godzilla's brother asks you to arm wrestle and you agree, that by itself is enough to check your breath (and brain) for bubbles. So, if you have any questions about your sobriety and ability to drive, ask the bartender. It is his *job* to know if you are drunk, and he is charged by law to shut you off if you give indications of intoxication. Ha! That means four or five drinks and everyone is shut off, little guys go down even sooner. It comes back to the same problem. A marginal drinker can't know when to say legally when and the bartender can't help him

Bartender: "Wonder if he's drunk. Let's see, that's his fourth, no I think his fifth beer, but they were all light beers. So, let me see, that's uh, five times twelve ounces... damn, I better figger this out on paper. Five times twelve, that's ought carry the two, add 'em all up, okay. That's seventy-two ounces. Now comes the hard part. Light beer is about 3.2 percent, he's uh about 160 pounds, looks like a normal, average man to me, apply Henry's law on alcohol concentration in the blood, that's average 2100 parts blood per one part booze. Uh... I forget, did he eat? Ah, bullshit. He ain't causin' no trouble, I'll give him another."

It's simple. If you don't know whether you are drunk, no one is going to tell you until it is truly obvious.

There is a cop in my town who is out to get me. He stops me for no reason, and last week he gave me the finger when we passed each other. What can I do about him?

For what they are worth, all cops have bosses. You have to complain. Every time a prick-cop hassles you on insignificant humbugs, you have to make an "official" objection at the police department. This sets the bastard up for a fall. (But *don't* argue with him at the traffic stop; you could get shot, or worse, you could make a fool of yourself.) "Overzealous" cops are everywhere, but they can be handled. A cop who regularly stops you for deminimis (chicken shit) violations is building a case against himself if you know how to work him up. Like a bounty hunter cop, the prick-cop must be more often right than he is wrong. Otherwise, he loses in court *as a routine*, his credibility fails and he and the municipality, county or state could be sued. Every cop must know the limits of his push. Even though the F.O.P. union will legally "defend to the end" all manner of police misconduct, there is a line where things become obvious. A cop with a record of a dozen or so stops of the same person in a year's time apparently has a microscope up the guy's ass. How much can you "serve and protect" the same individual on a regular basis? If you make an official report every time you are harassed, rousted or ambushed by this cop, the cop needs to show that he indiscriminately terrorizes everybody in order to show that he's not singling you out for harrassment. He can't do it, so you must report every stop, *especially* when you have done nothing wrong.

When you are sober, you should make a high-profile appearance, performing for the cop. Be legal, but drive past him about twenty times, honking, smiling and waving with all of your fingers. If you are not reckless, there is no law that says you can't be sociable. Cops love to be recognized; it's part of their training.

When you are drinking, however, the situation *demands* caution. First, as North Vietnamese General Giap advised: *Know your enemy.* Next, find him. You have to know what shift this cop works, what his detail is and where he is operating while you are out. If you can't pinpoint him, call the police department and ask: "Is Patrolman Bubble Butt on duty, I have some information for him?" When the dispatcher tells you that he isn't working until the 3:00 p.m. to 11:00 p.m. shift tomorrow, you know that you have a measure of relief from arrest. But... if he is working, then you must hide or divert him away from you. Hiding is easy, just stay in the bar until last call, then don't d..nk and drive. But diversion of the cop takes ingenuity. You can always call in a bomb scare on the other side of town. This tactic will surely suck all police units away from you. But this trick only works once. As soon as the cops recognize and pinpoint your call to a certain bar telephone (Star 69), they will just wait to roust you once you leave.

No matter how bad a cop is, he still works for the government, and governmental agencies hate lawsuits. Until recently, a lawyer only asked a victim of police abuse two questions: Did the cop strike you with his police car or did his police doggie bite you? Everything else was generally protected by immunity. Today, anybody can be sued anytime for anything... and governments, no matter how much they bluff, will often rather settle than fight.

You should know your enemy, know where he is, then avoid him. If all else fails, even if you are wrong, sue him. His prior record of harassment may convince his boss's lawyers to avoid court and settle your criminal charges with a mutual release.

One night last year I was charged with driving while intoxicated, driving under the influence, drunk in public, reckless driving, disorderly conduct, resisting arrest and spitting on the street. I threw up. The judge put me in jail for a month, I paid $1,500 in fines, lost my license for a year and had to go to 40 straight A.A. meetings. Now, a year later when I'm a respectable citizen, a sheriff arrested me at work for not paying fifty bucks for the disorderly conduct fine. It cost me another $200. Isn't that double jeopardy or something?

Even if it is double jeopardy, it won't matter much because the big charges against you have already been processed and settled. If a cop sprays you with a variety of charges at a drunk driving arrest, you want to plead guilty to the little charges up front, if allowed, and as fast as you can. If you can get a settled guilty plea processed for a charge like careless driving when this little charge *arises out of the same circumstances* as the drunk driving charges, you can get the bigger charges kicked out of court later as double jeopardy. This trick doesn't always work, but is sure worth a try.

Traffic cops generally use only two forms to charge you: (1) a traffic citation for speeding and lesser offenses or (2) a criminal complaint/information for the misdemeanor offenses like drunk driving. Often, the cop will charge you with two different traffic offenses on two different forms. The most common scenario is where you wreck after drinking and the cop issues a careless driving citation at the scene, then a few days later charges you with drunk driving. If you run to the municipal or magistrate's court and quietly pay the fine for the lesser offense, it is possible that the court system will digest your plea and forget about it. Now you have a merited adjudication that you can present to the trial judge at your later trial for drunk driving. You have already been sentenced, by paying a fine, for an offense rising out of the same circumstance as the drunk driving. Any subsequent trial for drunk driving based on this incident (wreck) should constitute double jeopardy.

Some prosecutors and state legislatures have become wise to this tactic, however, and require police to file all charges arising from the same circumstance on one and the same form when a drunk driving charge is involved. Police can just type in "careless driving," "disorderly conduct" or "too fast for road conditions," at the bottom of the pre-printed drunk driving form. With everything rolled together, you can't separate and plead out a lesser charge without the scrutiny of a judge or magistrate. In this way, the state is assured that you will be prosecuted *first* for drunk driving, which would render any later double jeopardy claim invalid.

Still, the little charges are important to the cop. If he didn't see you driving, he may need the lesser charges to establish probable cause for the drunk driving arrest. Two hundred feet of skid marks behind your car at an accident scene indicates speeding. You leaning against your wrecked car with a bump on your noggin indicates involvement, probably as the driver. Mix in "strong odor of alcoholic beverage" and the result is a tandem arrest for drunk driving and careless driving by speeding.

The cop has to write the little offense in order to charge the big one, and he must put both offenses on the same form if he wants to protect his arrest... And it is incredible how often he doesn't, even in the face of a state or district attorney order. Why? Usually because the cop is unsure of his stronger charge; or he is giving the drunk a break by writing a lesser charge, but his favor comes back and bites the cop in the ass when the drunk brags and a reporter investigates, so he now has to file a separate drunk driver charge; or the cop is lazy and doesn't want to type. Cop: "We got printed forms and we got citations. This asshole is gettin' a taste of both. It's good enough for government work."

Also, in some states' alternative sentencing programs, a drunk driving offense is not considered an adjudication, so if you opt for the alternative program, it doesn't matter what you did before with the lesser charges. You are going into a "program of rehabilitation" for your drunk driving charge. You are not being adjudicated guilty or innocent, so there is no defense of double jeopardy. Finally, in the case in question where a Deputy Dawg took $200 from you on an old $50 violation, as your lawyer I'd advise you to call the F.B.I. You will be doing a public service, as they need the work.

Sometimes when I drink beer I feel kind of woozy so I switch to rum or whiskey and coke, and I feel okay. If I switch my last few drinks, will that sober me up enough to drive?

No. It will certainly make your condition worse. While "beer on whiskey is mighty risky," cocktails after beer move you right into the fast lane. You don't need scientific evidence on this, just ask around the bar. Everyone has a war story. Their worst hangovers came from switching drinks, or drinking multiple exotic mixtures: A Brain (fish oil, Kahlua, gin, lithium); A Bullett (grain alcohol, moonshine, ginger ale, rat poison); a Blow Job

(Creme De Menthe, Creme De Coco, Brylcream, sperm whale extract). The danger always comes when you switch from milder drinks, like beer, to stronger ones, like Kamikazes. It is inevitable that the accelerated effect from stronger drinks will send you out crashing into the 7th fleet.

If you feel "beered out," you have been captured by the bloat. If you are driving, don't switch to anything but water. There comes a time in everyone's life when they have to grow up and take responsibility, no matter how much it hurts. But the good news is... there is always tomorrow.

Could you recommend some kind of a kit that people who drink and drive could put together to hide the effects of alcohol?

Sure. Start with Hall's Mentholyptus: don't leave the bar without it. You must mask the odor of the alcoholic beverage. Since alcohol itself has no odor, you could otherwise just drink straight gin because the flavoring is minimal, but that is still chancy. Stick with Hall's and keep sucking until you get home.

Next, you should have some wet-wipes, in case the cop chalked your car tires. They are also handy to wipe the bar stink off your clothes.

Take six to eight aspirin when finished drinking and a water bottle filled with ice and water for the ride home. The aspirin and ice will lower your body temperature and give a corresponding drop to your apparent blood alcohol reading. The water accelerates absorption and so speeds the booze out of your system. Additionally, it enhances cleaning of your mouth, teeth and throat. Booze can linger in your mouth long after you stopped drinking, particularly if you have dentures, caps or numerous fillings. That can lead to an artificially high alcohol reading on a breath test.

A couple B-12 vitamins will help wash the alcohol in the bloodstream. Take them early.

Sunglasses may not fit your apparel at midnight, but they are a sight better than the sore eyes you will be glowing at the cop.

Okay, any last questions?

So who is this "average" man that all these scientific guesses are based on?

If "average" is based on what there is the most of, according to one fabled trial lawyer, the average man is Chinese, he is named Mohammed and he is dead. There are more Chinese than anyone else, more guys named Mohammed and more dead people than living. That should give a little insight into the .10 percent "presumed guilty" drunk driving standard as a big lie, because the *per se* standard is based on a fictional "average" man. It's like asking a roomful of people, "What time is it?" You will get twenty different shades of what is really correct.

The mythical "average" blood alcohol standard was created from a lot of scientific and mathematical "averages" computed from a roomful of male test subjects who drank alcohol, then gave intermittent blood samples to a Swedish scientist, E.M.P. Widmark, in 1932. While the data suggests *some* basis for intoxication calculations, it doesn't work for everyone, all the time, in every circumstance. By his own admission, Widmark's theory is a guideline, not a definitive finger pointing at a specific blood alcohol percentage. Even though all states base their presumptive percentages for illegal drunk driving on Widmark's calculations there are a lot of reasons why Widmark's numbers don't necessarily lead to guilt in all cases.

For one thing, the averages have become grossly oversimplified through the years, where fixed but arbitrary set points have been established for a variety of factors: alcohol absorption into the blood, elimination from the blood over time, even body temperature set at a constant 98.6 degrees. These average "set points" disregard the wide range of data supplied by Widmark's test subjects: all men who were given fixed amounts of brandy or cognac over a period of hours, on an empty stomach. While Widmark cautioned that his data was supplying a "range of probable blood alcohol levels," today's experts have nailed down an "average" of the range and produced it as an exact proof of intoxication in a criminal trial, even though proof beyond a *reasonable* doubt is required to convict anybody of any crime in a democratic society.

Think of this: A diabetic woman who had one drink a half hour after consuming a full meal and then took four aspirin with several glasses of water which lowered her body temperature by 2 degrees and reduced her apparent alcohol reading, could still be "proved" as an "average" drunk an hour later by a breath machine that is programmed with data based on *male* alcohol consumption on an *empty* stomach and an average body temperature of 98.6 degrees and no consideration of illness. In that case, she could pay an "average" fine of $750, do an "average" 5 days in jail, lose her driver's license for an "average" 3 months and serve an "average" of 9 months on probation. Now that's a conviction according to the law of averages.

Let's look at a few more "average" numbers taken from Widmark's study. The absorption rate of alcohol into the bloodstream is pegged at an "average" .68 percent. This is the "average" ratio of the concentration of alcohol by weight in the body to the concentration of alcohol by weight in the bloodstream. This magic "average" ratio is the key to unlocking today's "experts's" blood alcohol content presumptions. Of Widmark's 30 test subjects, not one hit the .68 percent "average" on the button. Three people tested between .65 percent and .70 percent, nineteen were below .65 percent and eight were above .70 percent. Add to this the idea that no two stomachs are alike, alcohol purging rates may differ wildly, some people are ill when they test, men, women, fat and skinny people are going to metabolize alcohol in differing ratios... then what does a single blow into a breath machine prove? At best, maybe, all things considered, perhaps, well, it might, could be that the guy was drunk *when* he was driving... but then again, maybe not.

Still, every state in the union and every province in Canada presumes you guilty if your blood alcohol concentration is above a certain level. Yet the level as applied to individuals is arbitrary, "average" and very often plain wrong.

Can you beat a breathalyzer test? My friend says if you put a penny in your mouth, it neutralizes the alcohol readings. Is he right?

No. Your friend must have been sucking on lead pennies; it's made him a little simple.

Even so, there is a lot of voodoo in blood alcohol testing, particularly in breath testing. When you recognize that the air sample is just a tiny amount absorbed from the whole breath sample, you can see that there is room for error. Even though the machines are manufactured to specifically react to alcohol only, many are affected by smoke, cotton dust or tobacco and give unreliable readings. That is why the police are supposed to watch you for about twenty minutes before you test so that they know your mouth is empty and you can give a clean test. Still... it often happens that somebody blows their Copenhagen down the tube and knocks the machine out of service for about a month. Cops get bored real fast when they only have one job to do.

The machine's plumbing often causes unreliable readings as well. If the tubes leak and the breath sample, the preservative, chemical components or refrigerant in the system escapes, the test is worthless. What is worse is when the cop realizes that the machine is malfunctioning. In a futile attempt to save his arrest, the cop performs "home repairs" with tape or bubble gum or (I've seen this) a condom. At least the next drunk in line won't have to worry about getting AIDS.

Since the air sample is so important to the breath machine, you want to make sure that you offer the air that is most favorable to your circumstance. It is possible to blow around the mouthpiece by first sticking the tip of your tongue in the mouthpiece hole when blowing, then removing it to offer the very end of your breath sample. This "last" air should be about 4 degrees cooler than your body temperature and will result in a dramatically reduced alcohol reading. In dealing with government, sometimes it's not "who you know, but *how* you blow."

My friend told me that if the cops are watching T.V., it screws up the breathalyzer. Izatso?

On this one, your friend may be correct. Radio frequency interference (R.F.I.) affects almost all breath machines, unless they are properly shielded from the electronic transmissions, and has been cause to dismiss thousands of drunk driving arrests in this country.

The interference causes substantial variation and error in breath test readings and may derive from simple police radios, televisions, AM-FM radios, even clocks.

When you are taken in for a breath test, *look around!* But be quiet about it. Eyeball everything that ticks, buzzes, rings, whirls or whizzes, then tell your lawyer after you are released. In the cosmic sense, everything gives off radiation. Your test reading might be vaporized even if the cops aren't watching *The Munsters.*

Hey! Did I miss the Munsters?

Alright! You woke up. Don't worry. It's all in the hand out sheet titled *100 Rules of the Road.* You can get it on the way out. It gives you a short cut on everything we've covered. Good luck and please drive with your eyes open. If you can't, get some super glue... and don't sniff it!

Everybody else, stick around. We can do a happy hour until he is long out of the parking lot.

100 RULES OF THE ROAD

1. Don't drink and drive (you might spill your drink).

2. Don't drink *while* you drive. If it's not illegal, it's still dumb.

3. Don't make an arrest easy for the cop. Refer to #2.

4. If you must drink while driving, cover up the booze in a *closed* container when stopped.

5. Don't pick your nose on a bumpy road.

6. Don't smoke. Don't take dope. Don't jump rope.

7. Smokers are likely to have higher breath test readings.

8. If you dope and drive, don't take a blood or pee test. Take a breath test *only*.

9. Stop at yellow lights. The crossing car is always jumping on green.

10. Get the #?★! out of the passing lane.

11. Don't take a field sobriety test.

12. Take a chemical test unless...
    a) Someone may die from a wreck.
    b) This is not your first arrest.

13. Don't argue with the cop. He has a gun.

14. Call a lady cop "officer," not "toots."

15. Get a lawyer *experienced* with drunk driving cases.

16. If you do a breath test, take the mouthpiece and give it to your lawyer.

17. If you do any chemical test, ask whoever is in charge (nurse, doctor, sergeant) to preserve the test sample.

18. Don't try to talk your way out of a drunk driving arrest.

19. Mouth gets you into trouble, rarely out of trouble... SSSSSH!

20. If it ain't broke, don't fix it.

21. If you try, don't talk to the F.B.I.

22. *Never* talk to a news reporter.

23. ...Unless the cops, your lawyer or a volunteer is trying to have you killed.

24. Never waive a preliminary hearing.

25. If it ain't broke, don't fix it... But if you must, pay by check.

26. Save receipts, attorney cards or handwritten information, but keep your *own* fingerprints off them.

27. Never tell your lawyer more than he can find out for himself.

28. ...And keep both hands on your wallet and both eyes on your doggie.

29. Anything will burn if it gets hot enough. You too, no matter how important you are.

30. Remember at a traffic stop: All the best actors aren't in Hollywood. *Act sober!*

31. If arrested, know that all the right answers aren't in libraries... But, be careful.

32. Never consent to a cop search, even if you are legal.

33. Don't let another drunk drive your car. He could get you both put in jail.

34. If you are involved in an accident involving injuries or death, do the right thing. STOP!

35. Hall's Mentholyptus. Don't leave the joint without it.

36. Slow down. Bar clocks are always set ahead. You still have time.

37. We all swim in the same water: cops, robbers or news reporters...

38. But big fish still eat little fish...

39. Even though little fish still have rights.

40. Know yours, but don't make a big deal out of it.

41. You still have the right to remain silent... SSSSSH!

42. A fish never got legally hooked with its mouth closed.

43. If you wreck without complications (no injuries, deaths or imminent danger to others), go home and report the accident when you are sober.

44. Don't wait around at a simple fender-bender and ask the cop to arrest you.

45. Don't go to the nearest bar after you wreck. The cops surely will.

46. If you go home, stay *inside*. Don't answer the door, it's not a candy gram. Don't even go out on your porch.

47. Slow down in town, and don't drive on the sidewalk.

48. Don't drink and drive with kids in the car.

49. Don't expect anyone but a cop or your wife to tell you that you are drunk. Your "friends" will tell you to have one more.

50. If you burp, barf or belch during a breath test, STOP! You are giving stomach air which is much higher in alcohol content than lung air. Wait awhile then re-test.

51. The District Attorney only wants to see that a fair trial is conducted, right?

52. HA!

53. All work and no shirk makes Jack a dull off... until he starts partying.

54. Beware of amateur drunk drivers, they give professionals a bad name.

55. You can beat your meat, but nothing beats a Bud.

56. Know when to say when... about 5 o'clock. Then comes Miller Time.

57. If a breath machine says it is "O.K." before the test starts, don't believe it.

58. Don't trust the cop either. Watch carefully.

59. Supply enough air for the breath test, but make it the last part of your breath. It will be lower in alcohol content.

60. Eat. Almost any food is better than no food when drinking.

61. If you drink Kamikazes, ground your airplane or you might crash into the 7th fleet.

62. Drive with your window down. Out goes the bad air, in comes the good air.

63. Take four aspirin and four glasses of water before you leave the bar.

64. Check your tires for chalk marks and your trousers or dress for pecker tracks.

65. Be cool. Lower body temperatures give lower blood alcohol readings.

66. Life is cheap, but death is expensive. Stay alert or don't drive.

67. If you have been drinking, stay off the freeway, for Christ's sake.

68. If you drink and drive, don't carry a gun... not even in California.

69. If you sleep in your car, make sure it is off the road, with the engine off, then get in the back seat and *hide* the keys.

70. Don't let anyone drink in your car while you drive, it is probable cause for a traffic stop.

71. *Always* have your cards ready.

72. When a cop waves you over, wave back, but use *all* of your fingers.

73. Almost 2 million people get arrested in the U.S. each year for drunk driving. That pegs your chances of getting caught at less than one percent (if you count non-drivers, like infants or Leon Spinks). But...

74. The law of averages always runs against the "average" man.

75. Vehicular homicide by any other name is murder and calls for a jail sentence.

76. If a judge sentences you to ten days in jail, don't tell him that you can do it standing on your head.

77. He will give you an extra ten days on your ass.

78. Judges invented arrogance. Call them "Your Honor," not "Your Honesty." In a pinch, "Your Majesty" will do as long as you don't preface it with "Yo!"

79. If you get hit by another drunk driver, wait until the cop shows up, then yell, "He's drunk!"

80. Turn your ★?#! lights on when driving at night.

81. If you drink and drive, and then see a cop, don't panic! He is there to serve and protect you.

82. If you panic, don't confess, "I'm drunk."

83. Things *can* go wrong with the cop's case.

84. There is a lot of voodoo involved in chemical testing.

85. Women on the pill can register higher blood alcohol levels. What is the alternative?

86. If Tarzan and Jane were Irish, Cheetah would be a designated driver.

87. Get your own monkey. It's cheaper than jail.

88. Don't let a M.A.D.D. judge ruin your day in court.

89. Think before you drink... *Plan* to be a reasonably prudent drunk driver.

90. It's O.K. to slash a menace drunk driver's tires. Your kids ride on the highways, too.

91. If you take a chemical test after a serious (death or injuries) accident, get a private test done as soon as possible.

92. The world may revolve around the sun, but the room will spin by itself when you lay down. How did you get home?

93. Bribes and threats work best when you know the right pressure points.

94. A lawyer sometimes doesn't need to know the law if he knows the judge.

95. If you run from a wreck, as your lawyer I advise you to start drinking heavily... then give yourself up.

96. If you like the way cocaine smells, wear sunglasses, and wipe your nose.

97. If a cop stops you, don't lick your nose with your tongue.

98. Get a badge. Influence peddling is the industry of the 90s.

99. Be polite. This is America. Ass-kissing wins awards. (This works for Canadians, too.)

100. See Rule #1. Read the book. Don't get caught.

APPENDIX

Alcohol and Drunk Driving Laws of The United States and Canada

All 50 states, the District of Columbia and Canada prohibit driving, riding or operating a motor vehicle while intoxicated or under the influence of alcohol or drugs. States or territories that have a chemical test law are indicated by their percentage of blood alcohol content where you are presumed intoxicated and guilty.

In Canada, there is a federal chemical test law with a presumptive level of intoxication of .08 percent blood alcohol content. You are further required, if ordered, to take a chemical test.

It is generally illegal in the United States and Canada for a motor vehicle driver to drink alcohol while driving, but it is permissible in many jurisdictions for occupants of the vehicle to drink while the vehicle is in motion.

UNITED STATES

Alabama
The presumptive level of intoxication is .10 percent and applies to driving or riding a motor vehicle, moped, bicycle or horse.

There is an implied consent law that requires you to take a chemical test by blood, breath or urine or lose your driver's license.

Alabama is a member of the Interstate Driver License Compact but an out-of-state driver may not automatically lose driving privileges for an implied consent refusal.

Accidents involving death or personal injury require an immediate stop at the scene and report to police. Accidents involving property damage above $250 require a report to the state within 10 days.

It is legal to drive in Alabama (wet counties only) with an open alcoholic beverage container within your vehicle.

The legal drinking age is 21.

Alabama law does not authorize a hardship "bread and butter" driver's license for convicted drunk drivers.

Alaska
The presumptive level of intoxication is .10 percent and applies to driving or riding a motor vehicle or moped.

There is an implied consent law that requires chemical testing or loss of driver's license.

Alaska has not joined the Interstate Driver License Compact.

Accidents involving death, personal injury or property damage exceeding $500 require an immediate stop and report to local or state police.

It is illegal to drive a motor vehicle in Alaska with an open container of alcoholic beverage within your vehicle.

The legal drinking age is 21.

Alaska authorizes a hardship "bread and butter" driver's license but a court order following a hearing is required to authorize a license for a convicted drunk driver.

Arizona
A blood alcohol level of .10 percent is considered unlawful and proof of guilt and applies to driving or riding a motor vehicle, moped, bicycle or horse.

The Arizona implied consent law requires you to take a chemical test by blood, breath or urine. A refusal will result in a suspension of driver's license. Arizona law now requires 24 hours incarceration for an implied consent refusal.

Arizona belongs to the Interstate Driver License Compact, but an out-of-state driver may not automatically lose driving privileges for an implied consent refusal.

Accidents involving personal injury or death require an immediate stop and report to local or state police.

It is legal to drive in Arizona with an open alcoholic beverage container within your vehicle, but the driver may not drink while driving.

The legal drinking age is 21.

Arizona has no hardship "bread and butter" license.

Arkansas

The presumptive level of intoxication is .10 percent and applies to driving or riding a motor vehicle or moped.

An implied consent law requires you to take a chemical test by blood, breath or urine. A refusal will result in a suspension of driver's license.

Arkansas belongs to the Interstate Driver License Compact, but an out-of-state driver may not automatically lose driving privileges for an implied consent refusal.

It is legal to drive in Arkansas with an open alcoholic beverage container within your motor vehicle.

The legal drinking age is 21.

Accidents involving death or bodily injury require an immediate stop and report to police with an additional written report within 48 hours.

Upon application and a show of "dire need," Arkansas issues a restricted "bread and butter" license to drunk driving offenders.

California
The presumptive level of intoxication is .08 percent or .05 percent for a minor and applies to driving or riding a motor vehicle, moped, bicycle or horse.

An implied consent law requires you to take a chemical test by blood, breath or urine. A refusal will result in a suspension of driver's license.

California has adopted the Interstate Driver License Compact, but an out-of-state driver may not automatically lose driving privileges for an implied consent refusal.

Accidents involving personal injury or death require an immediate stop and report to local or state police. Accidents above $500 must be reported within 10 days.

It is illegal to drive in California with an open alcoholic beverage container within a personal or rented motor vehicle, but motor homes and taxis are exempted.

The legal drinking age is 21.

California now allows issuance of a restricted driver's license to a person whose driver's privilege would otherwise be suspended or revoked after a court order for drunk driving.

Colorado
The presumptive level of intoxication is .10 percent. With percentages of .05 percent to .09 percent you are presumed to be driving while ability impaired as a lesser offense. This standard applies to a motor vehicle, moped, bicycle or horse.

Colorado has an *expressed* consent law (you must nod your head). Refusal of a chemical test or registering above .10 percent requires a mandatory revocation of driver's privileges

Colorado belongs to the Interstate Driver License Compact, but an out-of-state driver may not automatically lose driving privileges for an implied consent refusal.

All accidents must be reported to state or local police immediately. Telephonic service is okay.

It is legal to drive in Colorado with an open alcoholic beverage container within your vehicle, but the driver may not drink while driving.

The legal drinking age is 21.

Colorado has a hardship "bread and butter" license, but it is not authorized for convicted drunk drivers.

Connecticut

Connecticut has a per se (presumptive) statute where you are guilty of drunk driving if registering a blood alcohol level of .10 percent or greater. This law applies to motor vehicles, mopeds, bicycles and horses.

There is an implied consent law that requires you to take a chemical test or lose your driver's license.

Connecticut is a member of the Nonresident Violator Compact, but an out-of-state driver may not automatically lose driving privileges for an implied consent refusal.

You are required to stop immediately and give information at accidents involving death or personal injury. Property damage in excess of $600 to any one person must be reported to the state within 5 days.

Transporting an open alcoholic beverage container in a motor vehicle is permissible unless the driver is under 21 years of age. A motor vehicle driver may not drink while driving.

The legal drinking age is 21.

Connecticut does not have a hardship "bread and butter" license.

Delaware

The presumptive level of intoxication is .10 percent with an immediate license suspension and applies to driving or riding a motor vehicle, moped, bicycle or horse.

There is an implied consent law where you are required to take a chemical test or lose your driver's license.

Delaware is a member of the Interstate Driver License Compact, but an out-of-state driver may not automatically lose driving privileges for an implied consent refusal.

Accidents involving death or personal injury require an immediate stop at the scene. Property damage above $500 must be reported immediately to local police.

A driver may transport, but not drink from, an open alcoholic beverage container within a motor vehicle.

The legal drinking age is 21.

Delaware issues a hardship "bread and butter" license to a driver who has been suspended on discretionary grounds. Since a drunk driving conviction requires a mandatory license suspension, a hardship license is not available to Delaware drivers convicted of drunk driving.

District of Columbia

The presumptive level of intoxication is .10 percent. You are considered "under the influence" as a lesser offense at .05 percent.

There is an implied consent law where you are required to take a chemical test by blood, breath or urine or lose your driver's license.

The District of Columbia is a member of the Nonresident Violator Compact, but an out-of-state driver may not automatically lose driving privileges for an implied consent refusal.

Accidents involving death or personal injury require an immediate stop at the scene. "Material" property damage must be reported to police at once.

It is illegal for anyone to drink within a motor vehicle or for the driver to transport any open alcoholic beverage container.

The legal drinking age is 21.

The District of Columbia has a vaguely outlined hardship "bread and butter" license which takes into account need, good character, past driving habits and public safety concerns. A hearing and order is required before the license department. A hardship license for convicted drunk drivers has not been specifically prohibited.

Florida

The presumptive level of intoxication is .10 percent and applies to driving or riding a motor vehicle, moped, bicycle or horse.

There is an implied consent law that requires you to take a blood, breath or urine test or lose your driver's license.

Florida is a member of the Interstate Driver License Compact, but an out-of-state driver may not automatically lose driving privileges for an implied consent refusal.

Accidents involving death, personal injury or property damage require an immediate stop at the scene and notice to the police, sheriff or highway patrol.

It is illegal to drive in Florida with an open alcoholic beverage container within a motor vehicle, but motor homes and taxis are exempted.

The legal drinking age is 21.

A hardship "bread and butter" license for convicted drunk drivers (or model glue abusers) is available in Florida by order of court if the applicant has successfully completed a driver improvement course for the rehabilitation of drunk drivers. A hardship license is prohibited for repeat offenders or for drivers who refuse to take a chemical test.

Georgia

The presumptive level of intoxication is .10 percent and applies to anything but trains.

There is an implied consent law for motor vehicles that requires you to take a chemical test by blood or breath or lose your driver's license.

Georgia is a member of the Nonresident Violator Compact, but an out-of-state driver may not automatically lose driving privileges for an implied consent refusal.

Accidents involving death or personal injury require an immediate stop at the scene and report to police. Accidents involving property damage in excess of $250 require immediate notice to police.

A driver may generally transport an open alcoholic beverage container within a motor vehicle. (Some local municipalities may prohibit this.)

The legal drinking age is 21.

Georgia law provides for the issuance of a hardship "bread and butter" license on the basis of "extreme hardship" for a driver who has been convicted for a *first offense only* while driving under the influence of alcohol or drugs.

Hawaii

The presumptive level of intoxication is .10 percent by weight of alcohol in blood and applies to driving or riding a motor vehicle, moped, bicycle or horse.

There is an implied consent law that requires you to take a chemical test or lose your driver's license.

Hawaii is a member of the Interstate Driver License Compact, but an out-of-state driver may not automatically lose driving privileges for an implied consent refusal.

Accidents involving death or personal injury require an immediate stop at the scene and report to the county police. Accidents involving property damage in excess of $1000 require immediate notice to police.

It is illegal to drive with an open alcoholic beverage container within your motor vehicle.

The legal drinking age is 21.

Hawaii law does not authorize a hardship "bread and butter" driver's license.

Idaho

The presumptive level of intoxication is .10 percent and applies to driving or riding a motor vehicle, moped, bicycle or horse.

There is an implied consent law that requires you to take a chemical test by blood, breath, urine or saliva or lose your driver's license.

Idaho is a member of the Interstate Driver License Compact, but an out-of-state driver may not automatically lose driving privileges for an implied consent refusal.

Accidents involving death or personal injury require an immediate stop at the scene and notice to police. Accidents involving damage to the property of any one person in excess of $750 require notice to police by the quickest means of communication available.

It is illegal to drive with an open alcoholic beverage container within your vehicle.

The legal drinking age is 21.

A hardship "bread and butter" driver's license is authorized for a convicted drunk driver unless also convicted for vehicular homicide.

Illinois

The presumptive level of intoxication is .10 percent and applies to driving or riding a motor vehicle or moped.

There is a tough implied consent law that requires you to take a chemical test by blood, breath or urine. This test is compulsory on the order of a police officer. Refusal can be construed as a separate criminal offense resulting in loss of driver's license, fines and jail.

Illinois is a member of the Interstate Driver License Compact, but an out-of-state driver may not automatically lose driving privileges for an implied consent refusal (but may be jailed on a separate charge).

Accidents involving death or personal injury require an immediate stop at the scene and notice to police. Accidents involving property damage in excess of $250 to one person's property must be reported to the nearest police department immediately. Accident reports may be required of passengers.

It is illegal to drive with an open alcoholic beverage container within your vehicle.

The legal drinking age is 21.

Illinois law authorizes the issuance of a hardship "bread and butter" driver's license for convicted drunk drivers upon a showing of "undue hardship." The applicant may be required to undergo a rehabilitative schooling program. A hardship license is also available for persons who have refused a chemical test under the implied consent law.

Indiana
The presumptive level of intoxication is .10 percent and applies to driving or riding a motor vehicle, moped, bicycle or horse.

There is an implied consent law that requires you to take a chemical test by blood, breath or urine or lose your driver's license.

Indiana is a member of the Interstate Driver License Compact, but an out-of-state driver may not automatically lose driving privileges for an implied consent refusal.

Accidents involving death or personal injury require an immediate stop at the scene and notice to police by the quickest means of communication. Accidents resulting in $750 or more in damage must be reported to state police within 5 days.

It is legal to drive in Indiana with an open alcoholic beverage container within your vehicle.

The legal drinking age is 21.

Indiana law authorizes a hardship "bread and butter" driver's license for first time drunk drivers if they have not also been convicted of vehicular homicide.

Iowa
The presumptive level of intoxication is .10 percent by weight of alcohol in blood and applies to driving or riding a motor vehicle, moped, bicycle or horse.

There is a tough implied consent law where refusal to take a chemical test may result in a criminal arrest.

Iowa is a member of the Interstate Driver License Compact. An implied consent refusal may not automatically suspend an out-of-state driver's license, but may lead to a criminal arrest within Iowa.

Accidents involving death, personal injury or property damage require an immediate stop at the scene and notice to police. All other accidents must be reported within 72 hours.

It is illegal to drive in Iowa with an open alcoholic beverage container within your vehicle.

The legal drinking age is 21.

Iowa law provides for a hardship "bread and butter" driver's license on discretionary suspension. Drunk driving convictions require a mandatory suspension. No temporary or limited hardship license is therefore available for drunk drivers... BUT!... (1)

special sections regarding the cops' reasonable grounds for a drunk driving arrest or (2) colorable issues regarding a driver's actual refusal to submit to a test may influence a county court to not issue a temporary hardship license.

Kansas

The presumptive level of intoxication is .10 percent and applies to driving or riding a motor vehicle or moped.

There is an implied consent law that requires you to take a chemical test or lose your driver's license. In addition, Kansas has an implied consent preliminary breath test law that requires you to blow into a portable unit at the scene of the traffic stop.

Kansas is a member of the Interstate Driver License Compact, but an out-of-state driver may not automatically lose driving privileges for an implied consent refusal.

Accidents involving death or personal injury require an immediate stop and report to police. All accidents between two or more vehicles require an immediate stop and exchange of information with the other drivers. Apparent damage to property in excess of $500 requires a later report to police.

It is illegal to drive in Kansas with an open alcoholic beverage container within your vehicle.

The legal drinking age is 21.

Kansas law authorizes a hardship "bread and butter" driver's license by special order of the court for convicted drunk drivers.

Kentucky

Intoxication must be medically proved with a presumptive level of at least .15 percent blood alcohol content and applies to driving or riding a motor vehicle, moped, bicycle or horse.

There is an implied consent law that requires you to take a chemical test or lose your driver's license.

Kentucky is a member of the Nonresident Violator Compact, but an out-of-state driver may not automatically lose driving privileges for an implied consent refusal.

Accidents involving death or personal injury require an immediate stop at the scene and notice to police. Accidents involving property damage of $200 or more must be reported to the state within 10 days of the accident.

It is legal to drive in Kentucky with an open alcoholic beverage container within your vehicle.

The legal drinking age is 21.

Kentucky law authorizes a hardship "bread and butter" driver's license for convicted drunk drivers.

Louisiana
The presumptive level of intoxication is .10 percent and applies to driving or riding a motor vehicle, moped, bicycle or horse.

There is an implied consent law that requires you to take a chemical test or lose your driver's license.

Louisiana has adopted the Interstate Driver License Compact, but an out-of-state driver may not automatically lose driving privileges for an implied consent refusal.

Accidents involving death or personal injury require an immediate stop at the scene and notice to police. Accidents involving property damage in excess of $100 require a report to police by the quickest means available.

It is now legal to drive in Louisiana with an open alcoholic beverage container within your vehicle.

The legal drinking age is 21.

Louisiana law allows the issuance of a hardship "bread and butter" driver's license for convicted drunk drivers with the approval and order of the court. A hardship license will not be issued to any driver who has refused a chemical test under the state's implied consent law.

Maine

The presumptive level of intoxication is .08 percent and applies to driving or riding a motor vehicle or moped. A special section of the law as applied to "under 21" year old offenders requires a one year driver's license suspension at a level of .02 percent or more.

There is an implied consent law that requires you to take a chemical test or lose your driver's license, but a drunk driving conviction carries a mandatory license suspension anyway.

Maine is a member of the Interstate Driver License Compact, but an out-of-state driver may not automatically lose driving privileges for an implied consent refusal.

Accidents involving death, personal injury or property damage in excess of $500 require an immediate stop at the scene and report to police.

It is legal, if over 21, to drive in Maine with an open alcoholic beverage container within your vehicle.

The legal drinking age is 21.

Maine law authorizes a hardship "bread and butter" driver's license for first-time drunk driving violators as well as drivers who have refused a chemical test under the implied consent law, provided that such applicant has first successfully completed a rehabilitation program conducted under the auspices of the state.

Maryland

Maryland has two separate laws that apply to drunk drivers: At .10 percent blood alcohol content and above, a driver is presumed intoxicated; at .07 percent and above, a driver is presumed guilty of a lesser offense of driving under the influence. This law applies to driving or riding a motor vehicle, moped, bicycle or horse.

Maryland has an implied consent law where *all* drivers must take a chemical test by blood or breath or risk loss of their driver's license.

Maryland is a member of the Nonresident Violator Compact, but an out-of-state driver may not automatically lose driving privileges for an implied consent refusal.

Accidents involving death or personal injury require an immediate stop at the scene and report to police.

It is illegal for any driver to transport an open alcoholic beverage container within the vehicle.

The legal drinking age is 21.

Maryland law does not authorize a hardship "bread and butter" driver's license for convicted drunk drivers.

Massachusetts

The presumptive level of intoxication is .10 percent and applies to driving or riding a motor vehicle, moped, bicycle or horse.

There is an implied consent law that requires you to take a blood or breath test or lose your driver's license.

Massachusetts is not affiliated with the Interstate Driver License or Nonresident Violator Compacts.

Accidents involving death or personal injury require an immediate stop at the scene and notice to police. Accidents involving damage in excess of $1000 require a report to police within 5 days.

It is illegal to drink while driving in Massachusetts.

The legal drinking age is 21.

Massachusetts law authorizes a hardship "bread and butter" driver's license for habitual offenders of minor traffic laws but does not include a conviction for drunk driving.

Michigan

The presumptive level of intoxication is .10 percent and applies to driving or riding a motor vehicle, moped, bicycle or horse. There is a lesser offense of "driving impaired" with a legal presumption of .07 percent.

There is an implied consent law that requires you to take a chemical test or lose your driver's license.

Michigan is not affiliated with the Interstate Driver License or Nonresident Violator Compacts.

Accidents involving death or personal injury require an immediate stop at the scene and notice to police. Accidents with apparent property damage in excess of $200 require a report to police.

It is illegal to drive in Michigan with an open alcoholic beverage container within your vehicle.

The legal drinking age is 21.

Michigan law authorizes a hardship "bread and butter" driver's license for convicted drunk drivers by court order after a showing of necessity and hardship. This law also applies to drivers who have refused a test under the implied consent law.

Minnesota

It is illegal to drive and you are considered intoxicated at .10 percent or above in blood alcohol content and this results in a 90 day license suspension. This law applies to driving or riding a motor vehicle or moped.

If arrested, you must take a chemical test. Refusal leads to a one year driver's license suspension and possible criminal charges.

Minnesota is a member of the Nonresident Violator Compact, but an out-of-state driver may not automatically lose driving privileges in other states for a refusal or drunk driving conviction.

Accidents involving death or personal injury require an immediate stop at the scene and notice to police. Accidents involving apparent damage in excess of $500 require notice to the state within ten days.

It is illegal to drive in Minnesota with an open alcoholic beverage container within your vehicle.

The legal drinking age is 21.

Minnesota has a liberal law that authorizes a "bread and butter" driver's license for convicted drunk drivers.

Mississippi

The presumptive level of intoxication is .10 percent.

There is an implied consent law that requires you to take a chemical test or lose your driver's license.

Mississippi is a member of the Nonresident Violator Compact, but an out-of-state driver may not automatically lose driving privileges for an implied consent refusal.

Accidents involving death or personal injury require an immediate stop at the scene and notice to police. Accidents involving property damage in excess of $250 require a report to the state within ten days.

It is legal to drive in Mississippi with an open alcoholic beverage container within your vehicle.

The legal drinking age is 21.

Mississippi law does not authorize a restricted "bread and butter" driver's license for convicted drunk drivers.

Missouri
The presumptive level of intoxication is .10 percent and applies to driving or riding a motor vehicle, moped, bicycle or horse. At .13 percent or greater, your driver's license is suspended.

There is an implied consent law that requires you to take a chemical test or lose your driver's license.

Missouri is a member of the Nonresident Violator Compact but an out-of-state driver may not automatically lose driving privileges for an implied consent refusal.

Accidents involving death, personal injury or property damage in excess of $500 require an immediate stop at the scene and notice to police.

It is legal to drive in Missouri with an open alcoholic beverage container within your vehicle.

The legal drinking age is 21.

Missouri law authorizes a hardship "bread and butter" driver's license for first-time drunk drivers but prohibits a license for driving while under the influence of drugs.

Montana
The presumptive level of intoxication is .10 percent.

There is an implied consent law that requires you to take a blood, breath or urine test or lose your driver's license.

Montana is a member of the Interstate Driver License Compact, but an out-of-state driver may not automatically lose driving privileges for an implied consent refusal.

Accidents involving death, personal injury or apparent property damage in excess of $400 require an immediate stop at the scene and notice to police.

It is legal to drive in Montana with an open alcoholic beverage container within your vehicle.

The legal drinking age is 21.

Montana law authorizes a hardship "bread and butter" driver's license but it does not apply to convicted drunk drivers.

Nebraska
The presumptive level of intoxication is .10 percent and applies to driving or riding a motor vehicle or moped.

There is an implied consent law that requires you to take a blood, breath or urine test or lose your driver's license.

Nebraska is a member of the Interstate Driver License Compact, but an out-of-state driver may not automatically lose driving privileges for an implied consent refusal.

Accidents involving death, personal injury or property damage require an immediate stop at the scene and a report to the Department of Motor Vehicles within 10 days.

It is legal to drive in Nebraska with an open alcoholic beverage container within your vehicle.

The legal drinking age is 21.

Nebraska law authorizes a hardship "bread and butter" driver's license for drivers whose license has been suspended for a chemical test refusal under the implied consent law. There is no hardship license for convicted drunk drivers.

Nevada

The presumptive level of intoxication is .10 percent and applies to driving or riding a motor vehicle, moped, bicycle or horse.

There is an implied consent law that requires you to take a blood, breath or urine test or lose your driver's license.

Nevada is a member of the Interstate Driver License Compact, but an out-of-state driver may not automatically lose driving privileges for an implied consent refusal.

Accidents involving death, personal injury or property damage require an immediate stop at the scene and report to police.

It is legal to drive in Nevada with an open alcoholic beverage container within your vehicle.

The legal drinking age is 21.

Nevada law authorizes a hardship "bread and butter" driver's license for convicted drunk drivers after a one year waiting period.

New Hampshire

The presumptive level of intoxication is .10 percent and applies to driving or riding a motor vehicle, moped, bicycle or horse. There is an enhanced penalty for a blood alcohol reading of .20 percent and above.

There is an implied consent law that requires you to take a blood, breath or urine test or lose your driver's license.

New Hampshire is a member of the Nonresident Violator Compact, but an out-of-state driver may not automatically lose driving privileges for an implied consent refusal.

Accidents involving death, personal injury or property damage require an immediate stop at the scene of an accident.

It is legal to drive in New Hampshire with an open alcoholic beverage container within your vehicle.

The legal drinking age is 21.

New Hampshire law does not authorize a hardship "bread and butter" driver's license.

New Jersey

The presumptive level of intoxication is .10 percent and applies to driving or riding a motor vehicle, moped, bicycle or horse.

There is an implied consent law that requires you to take a blood, breath or urine test or lose your driver's license.

New Jersey is a member of the Nonresident Violator Compact, but an out-of-state driver may not automatically lose driving privileges for an implied consent refusal.

Accidents involving death, personal injury or property damage in excess of $500 require an immediate stop at the scene and notice to police.

It is illegal to drive in New Jersey with an open alcoholic beverage container within your vehicle.

The legal drinking age is 21.

New Jersey law does not authorize a hardship "bread and butter" driver's license for convicted drunk drivers.

New Mexico

The presumptive level of intoxication is .10 percent.

There is an implied consent law that requires you to take a blood or breath test or lose your driver's license.

New Mexico is a member of the Nonresident Violator Compact, but an out-of-state driver may not automatically lose driving privileges for an implied consent refusal.

Accidents involving death, personal injury or property damage in excess of $250 require an immediate stop at the scene and report to police.

It is illegal to drive in New Mexico with an open alcoholic beverage container within your vehicle.

The legal drinking age is 21.

New Mexico law authorizes a hardship "bread and butter" driver's license for convicted drunk drivers upon order of court.

New York

The presumptive level of intoxication is .10 percent with a lesser offense of driving "impaired" at .07 percent as prima facie evidence. This law applies to driving or riding a motor vehicle, moped, bicycle or horse.

There is an implied consent law that requires you to take two chemical tests by blood, breath or urine if drugs are suspected or lose your driver's license.

New York is a member of the Nonresident Violator Compact, but an out-of-state driver may not automatically lose driving privileges for an implied consent refusal.

Accidents involving death, personal injury or property damage in excess of $600 require an immediate stop at the scene and report to police.

It is legal to drive in New York with an open alcoholic beverage container within your vehicle.

The legal drinking age is 21.

New York law authorizes a hardship "bread and butter" driver's license, but the law does not apply to convicted drunk drivers or drivers who refuse an implied consent chemical test.

North Carolina
The presumptive level of intoxication is .10 percent and applies to driving or riding a motor vehicle, moped, bicycle or horse.

There is an implied consent law that requires you to take a blood or breath test or lose your driver's license.

North Carolina is a member of the Nonresident Violator Compact, but an out-of-state driver may not automatically lose driving privileges for an implied consent refusal.

Accidents involving death, personal injury or property damage in excess of $500 require an immediate stop at the scene and report to police.

It is illegal to drive in North Carolina with an open alcoholic beverage container within your vehicle.

The legal drinking age is 21.

North Carolina law authorizes a hardship "bread and butter" driver's license by order of court for first-time drunk drivers.

North Dakota

The presumptive level of intoxication is .10 percent and applies to driving or riding a motor vehicle, moped, bicycle or horse.

There is an implied consent law that requires you to take a blood, breath, urine or saliva test, and if requested, a drug screening test. Refusal results in a loss of driver's license.

North Dakota is a member of the Nonresident Violator Compact, but an out-of-state driver may not automatically lose driving privileges for an implied consent refusal.

Accidents involving death, personal injury or property damage in excess of $1000 require an immediate stop at the scene and report to police.

It is illegal to drive in North Dakota with an open alcoholic beverage container within your vehicle.

The legal drinking age is 21.

North Dakota law authorizes a hardship "bread and butter" driver's license for drivers who refuse a chemical test under the implied consent law, but does not authorize a license for convicted drunk drivers.

Ohio

The presumptive level of intoxication is .10 percent (any amount if under 18*) and applies to driving or riding a motor vehicle, moped, bicycle or horse.

There is an implied consent law that requires you to take a blood, breath or urine test or lose your driver's license.

Ohio is a member of the Nonresident Violator Compact, but any driver who refuses a chemical test will have his license on the spot seized by the arresting officer.

Accidents involving death, personal injury or property damage in excess of $400 require an immediate stop at the scene and report to police.

It is illegal to drive in Ohio with an open alcoholic beverage container within your vehicle.

The legal drinking age is 21.

Ohio law does not authorize a hardship "bread and butter" driver's license.

Oklahoma

The presumptive level of intoxication is .10 percent and applies to driving or riding a motor vehicle, moped, bicycle or horse.

There is an implied consent law that requires you to take a blood or breath test or lose your driver's license.

---

* Ohio's chemical testing law is especially dangerous for drivers under the age of 18. Zero tolerance means they can get whacked for cough syrup, breath spray or non-alcoholic chemicals on the breath that register positive for ethanol.

Oklahoma is a member of the Interstate Driver License Compact, but an out-of-state driver may not automatically lose driving privileges for an implied consent refusal.

Accidents involving death, personal injury or property damage in excess of $300 require an immediate stop at the scene and report to police.

It is illegal to drive in Oklahoma with an open alcoholic beverage container within your vehicle.

The legal drinking age is 21.

Oklahoma law authorizes a hardship "bread and butter" driver's license for drivers who refuse a chemical test under the implied consent law. Convicted drunk drivers do not get a hardship license.

Oregon
The presumptive level of intoxication is .08 percent, .04 percent for commercial drivers and anything above .00 percent for drivers under 18 years[*]. This law applies to driving or riding a motor vehicle, moped, bicycle or horse.

There is an implied consent law that requires you to take a blood, breath or urine test or lose your driver's license.

Oregon is a member of the Interstate Driver License Compact, but an out-of-state driver may not automatically lose driving privileges for an implied consent refusal.

Accidents involving death, personal injury or property damage in excess of $400 require an immediate stop at the scene and report to police.

---

[*] Oregon's chemical testing law is especially dangerous for drivers under the age of 18. Zero tolerance means they can get whacked for cough syrup, breath spray or non-alcoholic chemicals on the breath that register positive for ethanol.

It is illegal to drive in Oregon with an open alcoholic beverage container within your vehicle.

The legal drinking age is 21.

Oregon law authorizes a hardship "bread and butter" driver's license for convicted drunk drivers.

Pennsylvania

The presumptive level of intoxication is .10 percent and applies to driving or riding a motor vehicle, moped, bicycle or horse.

There is an implied consent law that requires you to take a blood, breath or urine test or lose your driver's license.

Pennsylvania is a member of the Nonresident Violator Compact, but an out-of-state driver may not automatically lose driving privileges for an implied consent refusal.

Accidents involving death, personal injury or where a vehicle is inoperable require an immediate stop at the scene and report to police.

It is illegal to drive in Pennsylvania with an open alcoholic beverage container within your vehicle.

The legal drinking age is 21.

Pennsylvania law authorizes a hardship "bread and butter" driver's license, but it does not apply to convicted drunk drivers.

Rhode Island

The presumptive level of intoxication is .10 percent and applies to driving or riding a motor vehicle, moped or bicycle.

There is an implied consent law that requires you to take a blood, breath, urine or body fluids test or lose your driver's license.

Rhode Island does not belong to a reciprocal driver license compact.

Accidents involving death, personal injury or property damage in excess of $500 require an immediate stop at the scene and report to police.

It is illegal to drive in Rhode Island with an open alcoholic beverage container within your vehicle.

The legal drinking age is 21.

Rhode Island law does not authorize a hardship "bread and butter" driver's license.

South Carolina

The presumptive level of intoxication is .10 percent and applies to driving or riding a motor vehicle or moped.

There is an implied consent law that requires you to take a breath test or lose your driver's license.

South Carolina is a member of the Nonresident Violator Compact, but an out-of-state driver may not automatically lose driving privileges for an implied consent refusal.

Accidents involving death, personal injury or property damage in excess of $400 require an immediate stop at the scene and report to police.

It is illegal to drive in South Carolina with an open alcoholic beverage container within your vehicle.

The legal drinking age is 21.

South Carolina law authorizes a hardship "bread and butter" driver's license for drivers convicted of drunk or drugged driving.

South Dakota

The presumptive level of intoxication is .10 percent and applies to driving or riding a motor vehicle, moped, bicycle or horse.

There is an implied consent law that requires you to take a blood, breath or urine test or lose your driver's license.

South Dakota is a member of the Nonresident Violator Compact, but an out-of-state driver may not automatically lose driving privileges for an implied consent refusal.

Accidents involving death, personal injury or property damage in excess of $500 require an immediate stop at the scene and report to police.

It is illegal to drive in South Dakota with an open alcoholic beverage container within your vehicle.

The legal drinking age is 21.

South Dakota law authorizes a hardship "bread and butter" driver's license for first-time drunk drivers and drivers who refuse a chemical test under the implied consent law.

Tennessee

The presumptive level of intoxication is .10 percent and applies to driving or riding a motor vehicle, moped, bicycle, boat or horse.

There is an implied consent law that requires you to take a blood or breath test or lose your driver's license.

Tennessee is a member of the Interstate Driver License Compact, but an out-of-state driver may not automatically lose driving privileges for an implied consent refusal, but a driver's license may be seized at the time of arrest.

Accidents involving death, personal injury or property damage in excess of $400 require an immediate stop at the scene and report to police.

It is generally legal to drive in Tennessee with an open alcoholic beverage container within your vehicle.

The legal drinking age is 21.

Tennessee law authorizes a hardship "bread and butter" driver's license for drunk drivers and for drivers who have refused a chemical test under the implied consent law.

Texas
The presumptive level of intoxication is .10 percent and applies to driving or riding a motor vehicle or moped.

There is an implied consent law that requires you to take a blood or breath test or lose your driver's license.

Texas does not belong to a reciprocal driver license compact.

Accidents involving death, personal injury or property damage in excess of $500 require an immediate stop at the scene and report to police.

It is legal to drive in Texas with an open alcoholic beverage container within your vehicle.

The legal drinking age is 21.

Texas law authorizes a hardship "bread and butter" driver's license for convicted drunk drivers.

Utah

The presumptive level of intoxication is .08 percent and applies to driving or riding a motor vehicle, moped, bicycle or horse.

There is an implied consent law that requires you to take a blood or breath test or lose your driver's license.

Utah is a member of the Interstate Driver License Compact, but an out-of-state driver may not automatically lose driving privileges for an implied consent refusal.

Accidents involving death, personal injury or property damage in excess of $400 require an immediate stop at the scene and report to police.

It is illegal to drive in Utah with an open alcoholic beverage container within your vehicle.

The legal drinking age is 21.

Utah law authorizes a hardship "bread and butter" driver's license for convicted drunk drivers.

Vermont

The presumptive level of intoxication is .10 percent and applies to driving or riding a motor vehicle or moped.

There is an implied consent law that requires you to take a blood or breath test or lose your driver's license.

Vermont does not belong to a reciprocal driver license compact.

Accidents involving death, personal injury or property damage in excess of $500 require an immediate stop at the scene and report to police.

It is legal to drive in Vermont with an open alcoholic beverage container within your vehicle.

The legal drinking age is 21.

Vermont law does not authorize a hardship "bread and butter" driver's license.

Virginia

The presumptive level of intoxication is .10 percent and applies to driving or riding a motor vehicle, moped, bicycle or horse.

There is an implied consent law that requires you to take a blood or breath test or lose your driver's license.

Virginia is a member of the Nonresident Violator Compact, but an out-of-state driver may not automatically lose driving privileges for an implied consent refusal.

Accidents involving death, personal injury or serious property damage require an immediate stop at the scene and report to police.

It is illegal to drive in Virginia with an open alcoholic beverage container within your vehicle.

The legal drinking age is 21.

Virginia law does not authorize a hardship "bread and butter" driver's license.

Washington

The presumptive level of intoxication is .10 percent and applies to driving or riding a motor vehicle, moped, bicycle or horse.

There is an implied consent law that requires you to take a blood or breath test at the officer's choice or lose your driver's license for one year.

Washington is a member of the Nonresident Violator Compact, but an out-of-state driver may not automatically lose driving privileges for an implied consent refusal.

Accidents involving death, personal injury or property damage in excess of $500 require an immediate stop at the scene and report to police.

It is illegal to drive in Washington with an open alcoholic beverage container within your vehicle.

The legal drinking age is 21.

Washington law authorizes a hardship "bread and butter" driver's license for convicted drunk drivers and drivers who refuse a chemical test under the implied consent law.

West Virginia
The presumptive level of intoxication is .10 percent and applies to driving or riding a motor vehicle, moped, bicycle or horse.

There is an implied consent law that requires you to take a blood or breath test or lose your driver's license.

West Virginia is a member of the Nonresident Violator Compact, but an out-of-state driver may not automatically lose driving privileges for an implied consent refusal.

Accidents involving death, personal injury or property damage in excess of $250 require an immediate stop at the scene and report to police.

It is illegal to drive in West Virginia with an open alcoholic beverage container within your vehicle.

The legal drinking age is 21.

West Virginia law authorizes a hardship "bread and butter" driver's license for convicted drunk drivers.

Wisconsin

The presumptive level of intoxication is .10 percent and applies to driving or riding a motor vehicle, moped, bicycle or horse.

There is an implied consent law that requires you to take a blood, breath or urine test or lose your driver's license.

Wisconsin does not belong to a reciprocal driver license compact.

Accidents involving death, personal injury or property damage in excess of $500 require an immediate stop at the scene and report to police.

It is illegal to drive in Wisconsin with an open alcoholic beverage container within your vehicle.

The legal drinking age is 21.

Wisconsin law authorizes a hardship "bread and butter" driver's license for convicted drunk drivers.

Wyoming

The presumptive level of intoxication is .10 percent and applies to driving or riding a motor vehicle, moped, bicycle or horse.

There is an implied consent law that requires you to take a blood, breath or urine test or lose your driver's license.

Wyoming is a member of the Interstate Driver License Compact, but an out-of-state driver may not automatically lose driving privileges for an implied consent refusal.

Accidents involving death, personal injury or property damage in excess of $500 require an immediate stop at the scene and report to police.

It is generally legal to drive in Wyoming with an open alcoholic beverage container within your vehicle.

The legal drinking age is 21.

Wyoming law authorizes a hardship "bread and butter" driver's license for convicted drunk drivers.

CANADA

Alberta
The presumptive level of intoxication is .08 percent.

There is an implied consent law that requires you to take a breath test or lose your driver's license.

The United States and Canada have no reciprocal compact affecting their driving laws.

Accidents involving death, personal injury or property damage in excess of $1000 require an immediate stop at the scene and report to police.

It is illegal to drive in Alberta with an open alcoholic beverage container within your vehicle.

The legal drinking age is 21.

British Columbia

The presumptive level of intoxication is .08 percent and applies to driving or riding a motor vehicle, moped, bicycle or horse, .05 percent suspends license for 24 hours.

Refusal to take a breath test may result in immediate seizure of driver's license.

The United States and Canada have no reciprocal compact affecting their driving laws.

Accidents involving death, personal injury or property damage in excess of $1000 require an immediate stop at the scene and report to police.

It is illegal to drive in British Columbia with an open alcoholic beverage container within your vehicle.

The legal drinking age is 21.

Manitoba

The presumptive level of intoxication is .08 percent and applies to driving or riding a motor vehicle, moped, bicycle or horse.

There is an implied consent law that requires you to take a chemical test or lose your driver's license.

The United States and Canada have no reciprocal compact affecting their driving laws.

Accidents involving death, personal injury or property damage in excess of $500 require an immediate stop at the scene and report to police.

It is illegal to drive in Manitoba with an open alcoholic beverage container within your vehicle.

The legal drinking age is 21.

New Brunswick
The presumptive level of intoxication is .08 percent and applies to driving or riding a motor vehicle or moped, .05 percent results in a 24 hour license suspension.

There is an implied consent law that requires you to take a breath test or lose your driver's license.

The United States and Canada have no reciprocal compact affecting their driving laws.

It is illegal to drive in New Brunswick with an open alcoholic beverage container within your vehicle.

The legal drinking age is 21.

Newfoundland
The presumptive level of intoxication is .08 percent and applies to driving or riding a motor vehicle or moped.

There is an implied consent law that requires you to take a breath test or lose your driver's license.

The United States and Canada have no reciprocal compact affecting their driving laws.

It is illegal to drive in Newfoundland with an open alcoholic beverage container within your vehicle.

The legal drinking age is 21.

Northwest Territories
The presumptive level of intoxication is .08 percent. There is an implied consent law that requires you to take a breath test or lose your driver's license.

The United States and Canada have no reciprocal compact affecting their driving laws.

Accidents involving death, personal injury or property damage in excess of $1000 require an immediate stop at the scene and report to police.

It is illegal to drive in the Northwest Territories with an open alcoholic beverage container within your vehicle.

The legal drinking age is 21.

Nova Scotia
The presumptive level of intoxication is .08 percent and applies to driving or riding a motor vehicle or moped.

There is an implied consent law that requires you to take a chemical test or lose your driver's license.

The United States and Canada have no reciprocal compact affecting their driving laws.

Accidents involving death, personal injury or property damage in excess of $500 require an immediate stop at the scene and report to police.

It is legal to drive in Nova Scotia with an open alcoholic beverage container within your vehicle *so long as* it is out of the driver's reach.

The legal drinking age is 21.

Ontario
The presumptive level of intoxication is .08 percent. At .05 percent, a 12 hour license suspension is imposed.

There is an implied consent law that requires you to take a chemical test or lose your driver's license.

The United States and Canada have no reciprocal compact affecting their driving laws.

Accidents involving death, personal injury or property damage in excess of $700 require an immediate stop at the scene and report to police.

It is illegal to drive in Ontario with an open alcoholic beverage container within your vehicle.

The legal drinking age is 21.

Prince Edward Island

The presumptive level of intoxication is .08 percent and applies to driving or riding a motor vehicle, moped, bicycle or horse.

There is an implied consent law that requires you to take a chemical test or lose your driver's license.

The United States and Canada have no reciprocal compact affecting their driving laws.

Accidents involving death, personal injury or property damage in excess of $1000 require an immediate stop at the scene and report to police.

It is illegal to drive on Prince Edward Island with an open alcoholic beverage container within your vehicle.

The legal drinking age is 21.

Quebec

The presumptive level of intoxication is .08 percent and applies to driving or riding a motor vehicle or moped.

There is an implied consent law that requires you to take a breath test or lose your driver's license.

The United States and Canada have no reciprocal compact affecting their driving laws.

Accidents involving death, personal injury or property damage in excess of $500 require an immediate stop at the scene and report to police.

It is illegal to drive in Quebec with an open alcoholic beverage container within your vehicle.

The legal drinking age is 21.

Saskatchewan
The presumptive level of intoxication is .08 percent and applies to driving or riding a motor vehicle or moped.

There is an implied consent law that requires you to take a breath test or lose your driver's license.

The United States and Canada have no reciprocal compact affecting their driving laws.

It is illegal to drive in Saskatchewan with an open alcoholic beverage container within your vehicle.

The legal drinking age is 21.

Yukon Territory
The presumptive level of intoxication is .08 percent and applies to all motorized vehicles.

There is an implied consent law that requires you to take a breath test or immediately lose your driver's license.

The United States and Canada have no reciprocal compact affecting their driving laws.

Accidents involving death, personal injury or property damage in excess of $350 require an immediate stop at the scene and report to police.

It is illegal (only within municipal limits) to drive in the Yukon Territory with an open alcoholic beverage container within your vehicle.

The legal drinking age is 21.

YOU WILL ALSO WANT TO READ:

☐ **58072 ASK ME NO QUESTIONS, I'LL TELL YOU NO LIES,** *by Jack Luger.* Subtitled "How to survive being interviewed, interrogated, questioned, quizzed, sweated, grilled..." shows you how to handle any kind of questioning, including police interrogations, job interviews, court testimony, polygraph exams, media interviews, and much more.. *1991, 5½ x 8½, 177 pp, soft cover.* **$16.95.**

☐ **40076 THE GET OUT OF JAIL FREE BOOK,** *by Maxwell Hutchkinson.* This book starts off with a spellbinding history of escape attempts. You'll be stunned at how simple some escapes are, and how simple-minded some of the attempts are. The author reveals all the tricks for escaping and staying free: how inmates get weapons, how they create diversions, how they get over, under and through the wall, and how they stay free once they make it to the outside. *1992, 5½ x 8½, 87 pp, heavily illustrated, soft cover.* **$10.00.**

☐ **88114 HOW TO BEAT "HONESTY" TESTS,** *by Sneaky Pete.* So-called "honesty" tests are now used widely by employers to screen applicants for jobs and to test current employees to see if they're harming the company. This book takes a close look at these tests. Most honesty tests are provided by three companies, and they have predictable patterns. This book will show you how they work and how to defeat their attempts to probe your psyche. *1989, 5½ x 8½, 46 pp, soft cover.* **$5.95.**

☐ **76041 THE OUTLAW'S BIBLE,** *by E.X. Boozhie.* The best "jailhouse" law book ever published — for people on the outside who want to stay there. This is a real life civics lesson for citizen lawbreakers: how to dance the fine line between freedom and incarceration, how to tiptoe the tightrope of due process. Covers detention, interrogation, searches and seizures. The only non-violent weapon available for those on the wrong side of the law. *1985, 5½ x 8½, 336 pp, index, soft cover.* **$14.95.**

....

Loompanics Unlimited
PO Box 1197
Port Townsend, WA 98368 **DD93**

Please send me the books I have checked above. I have enclosed $_____ which includes $4.00 for shipping and handling of 1 to 3 books, $6.00 for 4 or more.

Name_____

Address _____

City/State/Zip _____
(Washington residents include 7.8% sales tax.)